THESE GOLDEN DAYS

THESE GOLDEN DAYS

*AN ILLUSTRATED RECORD
OF AN
OXFORDSHIRE MARKET TOWN
FROM THE 1930's*

BY

MARJORY LESTER

*Ride a Cock Horse to Banbury Cross
To see a fine lady upon a white horse
With rings on her fingers and bells on her toes
She shall have music wherever she goes.*

THESE GOLDEN DAYS

Published by Marjory Lester 1992

Printed by
Cheney & Sons Limited
Banbury, England

'These Golden Days'
has been published as
a limited edition of
1,500 copies

Copyright © Marjory Lester 1992

All rights reserved. No part of this publication
may be reproduced, stored in a retrieval system,
or transmitted, in any form or by any means,
electronic, mechanical, photocopying, recording
or otherwise without the prior consent
of the copyright owner.

ISBN 0 9512127 1 0

Contents

	PAGE
List of Illustrations	vi
Map of Banbury	vii
Introduction	viii
Acknowledgement	viii

Chapters

I	Friends of Friends	1
II	'When it rained the Eglantine smelt so sweet'	6
III	'They had to tuck their skirts into their bloomers!'	10
IV	Neighbours	13
V	'Pineapple chunks 3½d, pink salmon 6d'	16
VI	'Chopin with silk ties'	19
VII	Bull's Milk	24
VIII	'Oh Valiant Heart'	29
IX	Butchers, Doctors, Undertakers	32
X	A Throne of White Flowers	42
XI	'Barmbry Cakes, Cegarets, Chocolets'	46
XII	Going, Going – Gone!	51
XIII	The Bearded Lady, The Fortune Teller and The Wall of Death	57
XIV	Unemployment, Urinals and Spiceballs	63
XV	The Prophet	71
XVI	The Party's Over but the Memory Lingers on	75
XVII	And They're Off!	81
XVIII	Trials and Tribulations	89
XIX	'Is There Anybody There?'	93
XX	Over Here	100
XXI	These Golden Days I Spend With You	106

List of Illustrations

1. Woodgreen, Broughton Road showing a garden party. The home of Mr and Mrs Gillett.
2. Sunday morning – Grimsbury Methodist Chapel, West Street.
3. St Leonards School, Middleton Road – the Gym class.
4. St Leonards Parish Church, Middleton Road – a wedding.
5. The Methodist Church and School Room, Marlbrough Road.
6. Stroud's Farm, 'Mild May', Banbury Lane, (Middleton Road).
7. RAC Scout Mr Franklin at Banbury Cross.
8. The County Garage, 12 Horsefair on the corner of West Bar.
9. Clark's Flour Mill, Station Road with the gypsies and the canal.
10. Outside the GWR Station, Station Approach, on a Winter afternoon.
11. Interior of GWR Station, Banbury.
12. London, Midland and Scottish Station, Merton Street.
13. Banbury Michaelmas Fair at night, the Town Hall, in the distance.
14. The Market Place showing a street market, held on Thursdays and Saturdays.
15. Cadbury Memorial Hall, Bridge Street, with a Hunt Edmund's Brewers Dray in the foreground.
16. The Struggler's Public House, Mill Lane, with Mr Soden the sweep with his pony and trap.
17. The Banbury Guardian Office, Parsons Street with Theodore Lamb playing his gramophone in the street.
18. Calthorpe Street – a Coronation Street Party for Elizabeth II.
19. Calthorpe Street – children playing in the road, with Mrs Cooper, in the distance, pushing her green bread-cart.
20. The White Lion Hotel, High Street, with Tom Page on his grey mare and Dickie Manning, the dwarf on the footpath.
21. The White Lion Yard, with the wisteria and the stables.
22. Corpus Christi – a procession from St Johns Church down to Banbury Cross.
23. Boxing Day Meet outside the Whately Hall Hotel, Horsefair.
24. Banbury Town Hall, Cow Fair. Hoods Ironmongers on the right, on the left, looking up High Street.

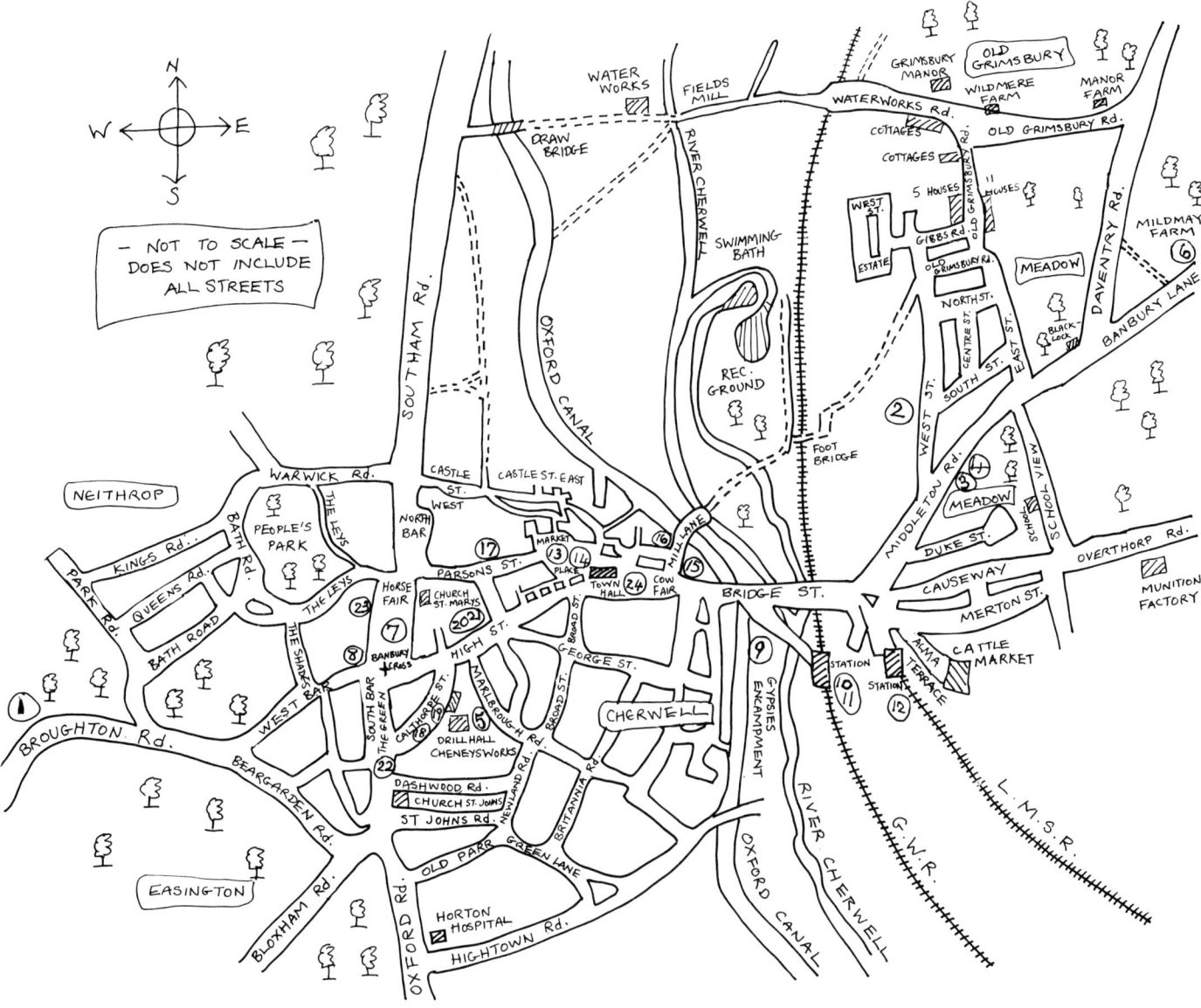

Introduction

The years between the two World Wars is a time I remember with great affection and though a time of hardships and great changes, it is a time I miss and regret the passing of – a lot of what was good is now lost. Many buildings, shops and streets are now demolished or in the process of disappearing as I write. Though they may not have been architecturally beautiful or important they are what gave the town its own particular character. If a stranger came to the area he would know Banbury was an Oxfordshire market town and not a town in Cheshire or Hertfordshire. There is now a uniformity in all towns where regional differences in food, dialect, buildings and customs are fast disappearing. I would never have thought in the space of my life-time so much would have altered.

This book is my personal recollections and how I saw the town. It is a follow-on to my first book 'Memories of Banbury', filling in more details of my past and memories of events, people and places which I have recorded in words and pictures. I apologise for any inaccuracy – my memory may be at fault.

But it is a personal view point.

"These Golden Days" is a keepsake I wish to leave to my family so they may know how difficult life was without washing-machines, no money, electricity and all the convenience foods and gadgets which are taken for granted nowadays. I don't want you to think I'm not for all these wonderful modern inventions but life seemed happier, and as for food – honestly it did taste better.

The sense of community spirit is no longer the same in Banbury of the 1990s and I know my feelings are shared by others.

I hope you enjoy this very personal, nostalgic gossipy journey through the golden days of my youth.

Acknowledgements

Mr Adkins; D. E. Andrews; Sir Adrian Cadbury; John Cheney; George Clark; Ted Clark; C. Cleaver; Mrs Elphick; Pamela Finding; Mrs Gurney; Mr Hutchings; Brownie Lay; Ernest Lester; Mr and Mrs Lord; Mark Soloman; Tony Sole; Mr and Mrs Stuchbury; Mr Tanner; Mr and Mrs Varnum; Peggy Watts

Lyric reproduced from 'The September Song' by kind permission of Warner Chappell Music Publishers Imp.

Also to all those who have kindly lent me photographs and their memories and for their help and encouragement and a very special thank you to my husband, Charles, and daughter Sylvia, whose collaboration has made this book possible.

I   *Friends of Friends*

I was born in Hackney in 1914. My parents were Quakers, Robert and Olive Pursaill and had met at the Peel Institute in Clerkenwell, St. John's Gate, London, a Quaker Welfare and Social Club. They came from very different backgrounds. Robert had been born in Peabody Buildings, Islington which had been built by an American philanthropist, to provide housing for poor families. When Robert was eight, his father died of drink, so he had to go to work selling newspapers to help support the rest of the family. At 18, a confirmed teetotaller, he joined the Peel Institute and because of the kindness shown him there, became a Quaker himself. The Institute was organised by Sir George Masterman Gillett, a wealthy London banker who originally came from Banbury. The house in Banbury where he lived, Charles and I were to buy nearly 50 years later.

The Club was run on non-sectarian lines as most of those in need were anti-religious and would have nothing to do with anything savouring of piety. As well as a Mother and Baby Guild at the Institute, there were social clubs and many other activities going on. A Quakeress, Doctor Richenda Gillett, gave her services. She had a close family connection with the Gillett family in Banbury. Sir George was very kind to my father and encouraged him to finish his education, to learn to read and write, to take a Pitman's secretarial course and take on the job as secretary and organiser of the male section of the club at a generous salary of £3 a week.

Olive, my mother, was the daughter of Doctor Thomas Chant and Mrs Laura Ormiston Chant, a well-known suffragette and Victorian social reformer. My mother was a worldly young woman who enjoyed theatres, dances and a social life. She had gone with her mother Laura to help out at the Peel Institute and was very moved by the dreadful poverty and suffering, especially of the women and children. Although not a Quaker at that time, she took a social worker's course at their college, Woodbrook, Selly Oak, Birmingham, to try to do something with her life, beside having a good time. After her course she was engaged by the Quakers to be the secretary and organiser of the women and children's section at Peel Institute.

She worked long hours, as the clubs were mostly held in the evenings and Sundays, while during the day there was the Mothers and Babies home visiting to be done. For the visits in Winter she wore a long white mackintosh, and in Summer a white dust coat as a protection from picking up lice and fleas, as most of the houses were infested with them. At the Mothers and Babies Guild the mothers were given advice and instruction to help them prepare for the coming baby and how to care for it when it arrived. The LCC sent speakers on health and hygiene and demonstrators who showed the mothers how to make baby clothes and make and trim pretty cribs out of orange crates. There were no such things as Mothercare shops, even if anyone could have afforded them. Materials were bought in bulk. The mothers put by a few coppers a week to pay for what they used, so that there was a nice layette, belonging to the mother, ready for the baby, instead of having the loan of a parish bundle of baby clothes, which would have to be given back at the end of a month. The babies were weighed and measured each week, with free

Virol and dried baby food being given out. The Virol was wonderful for treating and preventing rickets, from which nearly all the babies suffered. The manufacturers of Virol and several other baby food companies generously gave their products to help the mothers and babies at the club. It was an area of terrible slums, especially around Smithfield Market and a cheese factory nearby added to the stench. Infant mortality was appalling, not through lack of love but because of dreadful poverty, malnutrition and ignorance of how to care for a baby.

In 1913 my mother and father married. They lived in rooms at Sutton Place, overlooking St. John's Church, Hackney. My mother continued working part-time after I was born, always taking me with her to the Mothers Guild. However, when I was a few months old she had diphtheria very badly, so we moved to Prince Edwards Road, Carshalton, which was then almost in the country – we had a meadow at the bottom of the garden.

With the outbreak of the First World War, in 1914, my father a conscientious objector, had joined the Friends Ambulance Unit and was sent to France. My mother and grandmother Laura, who was living with us, took in eight girl Munition Factory workers, charging them only five shillings a week, full board. The girls earned very big money, about £8 per week, but couldn't do the work for very long as their skins turned bright yellow. After a while my mother and grandmother had to give up the house and the boarders, as it was hard work and costing them too much. After the war we came to Banbury in 1920.

My grandmother, Laura Ormiston Chant, first became concerned with 'Women's Rights' in 1878, when her first baby was born and she discovered that she had no legal right to the baby, only the father of a child had. In 1882 she and her husband moved to London, where she joined Josephine Butler's great work for 'Social Purity', as it was then called. Laura spoke everywhere, championing the cause, in spite of ridicule and abuse. The campaign was successful in winning a repeal of the 'Contagious Diseases Act'. Laura became involved in campaigning for the first Children's Act 1886 and in 1888 she made her first visit to America, as a delegate to the 'First International Council for Women'. She loved America and the Americans loved her and she made many trips there.

In 1894 she was asked to lead an appeal against the continued licensing of the Empire Music Hall. The Promenade in the theatre was used as a market for prostitution and no decent women or girl could go there without being propositioned. Vested interests were making vast profits from exploiting the women and were strongly against any change. She was chosen to lead the appeal as she had personal magnetism, great charm and wonderful eloquence. The Empire Music Hall was closed and all London went wild. Crowds gathered outside her home and effigies of her were burnt in the streets and she and her family had to have police protection. The BBC have several radio programmes, which they put out from time to time, in which she is depicted as a narrow-minded prig. This was untrue, as her only concern was in the exploitation of women.

Laura was a warm-hearted generous woman, small with an aquiline nose, large dark eyes, an abundance of dark hair and a fine ivory skin and dressed in beautiful clothes. Her husband, Doctor Thomas Chant, was the centre of her life and he gave her unfailing support in all her work. When he died the inspiration went out of her life. She was left with very little money and made her home with us in Banbury. She is buried at Sibford at the Quaker Meeting House even though not a Quaker but because of the great respect in which she was held.

Throughout my recollections Quakers or 'Friends' as they call themselves figure largely. They were not out to convert but to give generously of their time and money, to help where they felt there was a great need. In Banbury there was a large network of Friends who became our friends. The Town owes the Quakers a great debt for all they did and gave. One influential Quaker family was the Gilletts of Woodgreen.

Woodgreen, at the top of Broughton Road on the north side, was the home of Joseph and Beatrice Gillett. It had been built by Joseph's uncle, Charles Gillett and was a fine house set in a hollow with beautiful grounds and trees.

Joseph was a wealthy director of Gillett's Bank (now Barclays Bank) and every day he would go up to London by train. He had many interests and hobbies. When wireless was in its infancy he had a transmitting station at Woodgreen and would radio messages down to his brothers and sister in the attic of their home at 4 West Bar where they would try and pick up his faint scratchy messages. He studied the weather, was a geologist and in his small brickworks at the top of Broughton Road he experimented with making bricks with non-injurious materials, and from these bricks built the four houses beside the brickworks and two houses on the corner of Park Road. He had a small swimming pool and swam in it every day. The water was always freezing cold as it was fed straight from the stream running across his land. A strict vegetarian and teetotaller he was considered a health crank. Tall and thin, very generous, gentle and kindly – everyone liked him.

His wife Beatrice was short and stout with a beaming smile, which quite belied her character as she was narrow-minded and overbearing. But she was a caring person and busied herself with many charities and good works. Joseph always supported and financed her in any good work or charitable project she undertook.

When I was a child in the 1920s there was only a dental clinic for school children. There was however a Nursing Association, financed by annual private subscriptions, paid by women from all walks of life with whatever amount they could afford, as they were so grateful for its help. A fully trained nurse was employed and a house was provided for her by Beatrice, who would also make good any deficit at the end of the financial year. The nurse went to anyone who needed her, charging a fee of whatever the patient could afford. She was a smart young woman dressed in a navy blue uniform, with a white starched headsquare, and when out on her rounds she wore a cape with a grey veiling square pinned over her head, riding on a bicycle with a black bag strapped on the carrier. Beatrice also ran the Blue Bird Temperance Hotel in Bridge Street for commercial travellers so they had somewhere comfortable to stay, other than a pub. She provided a hostel for homeless girls, a pleasant house though strict, it was somewhere for them to go. For many years she was on the Town Council and served a term as Mayor.

Joseph and Beatrice always lent their garden and the three fine tennis courts for fêtes or tennis tournaments – any activity in aid of charity, with their drawing room always available for committee meetings. In my picture I have painted a garden fête in their garden which I remember so well. The fête is in aid of the 'Early Closures Association'. The Association was formed for shop assistants for better working conditions and shorter hours. The school children in the front of the picture are giving a display of country dancing with their teachers playing the piano. The minstrels were a local band of entertainers. The man in the hobby-horse costume is Mick Hawkins, one of the Association members. Joseph and Beatrice Gillett are the figures standing in the background on the terrace, dressed in brown. The Gilletts' big black car with the uniformed chauffeur, Mr Almond, standing by, is under the big cedar tree.

I wonder how many people in the town know that the paddling pool (now filled in as a sand-pit) and the Bandstand (now demolished because of vandalism) in the People's Park, were given by Joseph and Beatrice. The outdoor swimming pool in Park Road was also given to the town. The land around Woodgreen which they owned they sold very cheaply to the town to enable the new council housing estate – Bretch Hill – to be built. The Northern Aluminium Company, now 'Alcan', are in the town also because of Joseph and Beatrice. At the time the Mayor and the Town Clerk had persuaded Alcan to build their new factory in Banbury, with the council promising to forego any rates for several years. Mr Lidsey, the farmer who owned the land where the factory was to be built, however changed his mind on the agreed price for the land, suddenly putting up the price drastically. Alcan refused to pay and were withdrawing from the deal. The town was devastated, as industry was badly needed as unemployment was so high. To raise the difference the Mayor and several councillors generously gave large donations out of their own pockets, with Joseph and Beatrice saving the day by making up the balance of £500, which in those days was equal to the price of a good modern house. The deal was saved and Alcan was established in the town.

When Joseph and Beatrice died, they bequeathed their home and land to the town to be used as a school. It became part of the grammar school but later, a teacher named Mr Emmott begged to be allowed, as an experiment, to try running a technical school. Besides the usual subjects taught, the girls learnt book-keeping, shorthand and typing with the boys learning carpentry, metal work, technical drawing, painting and decorating. The school was a great success, fulfilling a need for preparing youngsters with a trade. The school closed when the Banbury schools became comprehensive. Since then, Woodgreen has become known as the Frank Wise School for children with special needs. Now, in spite of opposition, except for the house, Joseph and Beatrice's gift has been sold to a housing development which took away most of the lawns and many of the trees where the children enjoyed playing so much.

1. Woodgreen, Broughton Road.

II   'When it rained the Eglantine smelt so sweet'

In 1933 when I was 19, my father, mother and I moved to Grimsbury. We lived at 107 Middleton Road. When we moved in, the house had been empty for two years and before that it had been for some time a boarding house. Nothing had been done to it for ages so we managed to rent it for only £50 per annum. Once Grimsbury had been the best part of the town and there were still many fine houses and gardens but most of them had become shabby and run-down with many being let off in rooms or turned into lodging houses. The railway was nearby and it was noisy and everything got covered with soot. But away from it, there were pretty walks and the open countryside. 107, 109, 111 and 113 were a terrace of houses opposite a meadow. They had been built by brothers James and Joel Cadbury in about 1856 (a connection of the Cadbury Chocolate firm in Bournville). The fronts were identical but the insides were all slightly different and the long back gardens were different sizes and shapes surrounded by high brick walls. They had back entrances and double doors into South Street and halfway down the gardens, toilets, wash-houses and yards for drying laundry.

107 Middleton Road originally belonged to Mr Durrant, a well-to-do jeweller and a prominent member of the West Street Methodist Chapel. He had the best of everything for his house – fine marble fireplaces, the best fixtures, fittings, decorations, carpets, curtains and furniture, including a grand piano in the drawing room. He entertained the visiting speakers and leading members of the Chapel and often held social and musical gatherings in his house and garden. There were two large bedrooms on the first floor. The guests had the pleasant room at the back overlooking the garden and Mr Durrant occupied the splendid bedroom in the front. He had two massive mahogany wardrobes with bevelled glass mirrors built on either side of the marble fireplace and between his room and the guest room, installed a cloakroom with a grand toilet and wash-basin for his and his guests' exclusive use. His daughters and the maid had the two small back bedrooms at the top of the house.

Mr Durrant was a handsome man with white hair and a trim white beard. At home in the evenings he wore a velvet jacket with silk lapels and a velvet skull cap with a long silk tassel but he was a tyrant and ruled his household with a rod of iron. He had two daughters. The elder girl kept house and did the cooking while the younger worked in their Father's jewellery shop in the High Street. After his first wife died he remarried, as he needed a hostess for his entertaining and a chaperone for his girls. She was a refined lady who enjoyed ill-health and needed a great deal of waiting on. She had the big front bedroom on the second floot as a bedroom and bed-sitting room and was constantly ringing her bell, so that Miss Durrant, or the maid, had to run all the way up from the basement kitchen to the top of the house to see what she wanted.

When Mr Durrant died he left the house to his wife for her lifetime and on her death it was to revert to the West Street Chapel, to provide that Chapel with an income. The three women lived on in the house for several years until Mrs Durrant died and then the Misses Durrant had to move out. Although they resented the terms of their Father's

2. *Grimsbury Methodist Chapel, West Street.*

will they were glad to go, as they couldn't afford the upkeep of the house and the older Miss Durrant was having terrible trouble with her legs, caused by constantly going up and down the long flights of stairs. Mr Durrant had left the shop and premises to his daughters, so they went and lived above it. The elder Miss Durrant kept house while the younger sister, who had excellent taste and was a good business woman, ran the shop. She kept the shop stocked with attractive jewellery and fine silverware. If you wanted something special, you went to Miss Durrant's for it.

The Chapel Trustees found it hard to let the house as not many people wanted large Victorian houses, which were expensive to run and hard to heat and Grimsbury was no longer a fashionable area. People preferred the modern houses on Oxford or Bloxham Road. The Miss Durrants were delighted when we moved into 107 and we became great friends. Mother and I often called on them and they would tell us about their father, stepmother and the splendours of 107 in the old days. Sometimes they visited us but were always upset if we had made any alterations. After a year, as my father had spent a great deal on the house, the Trustees offered to sell it to him for £500 and provide a mortgage. Of course he bought it, but the Miss Durrants were furious amd kept sending him nasty letters demanding money for the mahogany wardrobes, cupboards and other fixtures and fittings. My parents were dreadfully upset and finally had to ask the Trustees to intervene.

Of the four houses, 107 Middleton Road had the prettiest garden, although it was not the largest. While it was standing empty the Trustees had had the grass cut, the trees pruned and the worst of the weeds pulled up but it was very neglected and my parents had to work hard getting it back into shape. The garden was in three sections and the house was the only one of the four with a side entrance and a piece of garden beside it. The side garden had a rockery with a large almond tree growing in the middle of it and every Spring the tree was a mass of pink blossoms which brightened up the whole road. Behind the house there was a large rockery made of ornately carved stones and on the top of the porch over the basement back door was an old tombstone with someone's name engraved on it. The stones were said to have come from the old St Mary's Church, which was demolished in 1790. There was an old lilac tree, masses of flowering garlic and bluebells and a huge Keswick Codling apple tree which every year was laden with large juicy apples. The bottom garden had two long paths with flower beds on either side. There were numbers of mature fruit trees, fruit bushes, flowering shrubs and many old and unusual plants. When it rained the Eglantine hedge smelt so sweet and on a summer evening the jasmine, which grew against the wash-house wall, filled the garden with its perfume. There were masses of snowdrops, violets, Christmas roses and large clumps of rare dark blue aconites. Someone however told my mother that aconites were poisonous and should be got rid of so she dug them all up. I thought it was a pity as I couldn't think of any reason why we should want to eat them.

My future husband, Charles Lester and I, decided to make a large pond in the middle of the garden. I tried to help him by mixing some of the concrete but it was too hard work for me, ruined my hands and the cement got in my hair. The pond was twelve feet across, ten feet wide, thirty inches deep and shaped like a figure eight. There were pockets and shelves for water lilies, a small island in each half of the figure eight and a bridge across the middle. We stocked it with threepenny and sixpenny fish bought from the local pet shop and from goldfish won at the local annual fair. It was a lovely pond and was overlooked by a pretty wooden summer house with a fluted pointed roof, a copper weather vane on the top and a deep purple clematis which climbed all over one side. Inside, the walls were large wooden panels, painted with romantic scenes of ladies and gentlemen in elaborate costumes. They had been painted by the younger Miss Durrant and the Curate of the Methodist Chapel. They spent a lot of time in the summer house as they were courting and engaged to be married. Sadly, the young man died and Miss Durrant never married.

Another time Charles and I made ten gallons of cider from the apples. First we minced them in an old mincing machine, then put the pulp into muslin bags and pressed out the juice with an odd contraption made from a trouser press, a car jack and two large square boards. It was very hard work and took us ages to fill up the ten gallon barrel. We added pounds of raisins, two bottles of rum and a large piece of raw steak, instead of the dead rat, which we were told we should have put in. Then we sealed up the barrel and let it stand for a year. I remember our disappointment when we first opened the barrel and found it was not sparkling and sweet like Bulmers Cider. It was still and a lovely golden colour but was very sharp and we thought it tasted nasty. However, our old weekly gardener said it was good and always asked for a glass of it with his mid-morning bread and cheese. Our big barrel of cider lasted for years, becoming more alcoholic the older it got. During the War when drink was scarce and hard to get we were glad of our cider, for when it was warmed and some sugar added, it made a strange, soothing and very potent drink.

III 'They had to tuck their skirts into their bloomers!'

Just across the road from 107 Middleton Road was a meadow and St. Leonard's Church and School. The old St. Leonard's School was part of the St. John Ambulance Brigade headquarters. Parts have been pulled down and the old asphalt playground is now covered with grass but in the main, the building is much the same.

The school was closed a long while ago as it was overcrowded and the buildings old-fashioned and not up to modern education standards. In spite of that it was a wonderful school with a fine staff who gave the pupils a sound basic education and plenty of opportunities for outside interests, such as music, drama, ancient history and nature studies.

There was Mr Spicer, the headmaster, who was popular with the pupils in spite of walloping them if he found them misbehaving, either in or out of school. He was very happily married with two little daughters whom he loved dearly. He was an energetic, jolly man and rode about at great speed on an old-fashioned push bike. There was Mr Burroughs, the assistant headmaster – a quiet man whom everyone liked. Miss Waters was another good teacher, who taught at the school for many years, living at 93 Middleton Road and dying when she was over a hundred years old. Mrs Varnum taught a class of younger children. She and her husband Jim and little daughter lived at 103 Middleton Road. Jim was churchwarden at St. Leonard's Church for many years. There was Miss Harris, who prepared pupils for the 'Scholarship' exam for which the school had a good record of successes. She lived in the village of Broughton and drove to school in a little Austin car. She wore sensible tweed skirts, woollen sweaters and stockings and good brogue shoes. Her short cropped hair was ginger and she was full of energy and enthusiasm. When she supervised the girls' games she used to dash about the playground shouting instructions or blowing a whistle. When they did PT she joined in with great vigour. The playground was a poor little place with only a high wide mesh wire fence between it and Middleton Road and it had to double as the games and PT area for the school. In those days shorts for girls were unheard of, so when they did games or PT they had to tuck their skirts into their bloomers. This was all right for the little girls but dreadful for the older girls who hated being seen like that as all the people passing in Middleton Road used to stop to watch. Sometimes the ball went over the fence and into the road or nearly hit the passers-by and had to be fetched back. Poor Miss Harris died of bowel cancer when she was barely middle-aged and although she suffered terribly she was very brave right to the end.

And there was also Miss Watts, who taught at the school for many years and although she was very strict the children liked her, calling her 'Watty' behind her back. She insisted that everyone could read and write properly and have a good grounding in arithmetic. Every morning her class would stand to attention and recite the multiplication tables in unison – parrot fashion. It worked and no one forgot their tables. Her great interests though were in ancient history and nature study and she would take groups of children on informal rambles to ancient historical sites or searching for nature study specimens which everyone enjoyed immensely.

Every year the school held a May Festival and at Christmas, a Pantomime. All the staff gave hours of their own time helping in these shows with everyone being responsible for some part and with Mr Spicer and Mrs Varnum directing the whole event. Mr Spicer was always the producer. For the May Festival he arranged the music and played the piano. For the Pantomime he wrote the script and all the songs which were full of allusions to local people and events. There was a part for everyone who wanted to be in the show. Mrs Varnum designed and made all the costumes. It was a huge task and she was busy sewing every evening and weekend, for weeks beforehand. As the school had very little money she used to rush up to the market during her lunch-time to buy cheap remnants of material and oddments of lace and ribbons for the costumes. They gave three performances of both shows which were always packed out and all the tickets sold. The shows were very popular. Most of Grimsbury liked to come and tickets were bought early or you didn't get in. When all expenses were paid there was usually something over for the school funds.

Mr Spicer and his staff knew most of the circumstances of their pupils' home lives so if there was any hardship they tried in a quiet way to help as much as possible. If someone's mother was ill and it meant the pupil staying at home to look after little brothers and sisters, Mr Spicer always let the little ones come to school and be in class with their older brother or sister or be looked after in the infants class, so as to relieve the pressure at home.

Mr Spicer's wife, Sylvia, died suddenly when she was a young woman, leaving Mr Spicer broken-hearted. He coped with bringing up his little girls by himself for a long time but he was very lonely and eventually married again.

Next to the school was, and still is, St. Leonard's Church and Hall. It was Grimsbury's Parish Church and like the Old Methodist Chapel in West Street had a large congregation and was a centre of the community. It was very High Church and beside the local congregation numbers of people came from other parts of Banbury as they liked the services. It had one tinny sounding bell which rang for all the services and funerals. Its mournful clanging seemed to go on for ever. But the bell had its uses, as we always knew when it was noon, as it rang twelve times for Angelus. The smell of the incense used to waft along the road, particularly at Easter time when they held long special services.

All the members took an active part in running the church. I remember Mrs Dwyer, the doctor's wife was organist, Jim Varnum, whose wife taught at St. Leonard's school was churchwarden for twelve years and Ferdi Warren the baker, was a sidesman. There were many others but I have forgotten their names.

The Church Hall was always fully booked for the Sunday School, Parish and Club Meetings and numerous other events such as Sales of Work and Jumble Sales. Every week in winter, Jack Friday and his popular dance band organised and played at the Saturday night dance. Jack lived at the top of East Street and his brother kept the off-licence lower down the street. The Hall was in great demand for weddding receptions, birthday parties and other celebrations and had to be booked well in advance.

On the right side of Middleton Road beyond the Church and Hall was a large meadow. On one side was the Duke Street tip, some allotments and the School View, Council School playground and on the other side the houses in School View. It made a very pleasant outlook for the houses on the opposite side of Middleton Road, as on sunny days the sun shone on it all day long and on winter mornings you could see the sun rising like a big red ball over the tops of the School View houses. The meadow had a strange undulating surface, almost like the waves of the sea. I think it is called Ridge and Furrow. It was a popular place for children to play and there were always crowds of them there. In Causeway and School View lots of men kept pigeons and it was a lovely sight to see the birds wheeling over the meadow when they were let out for their morning and evening flights. It was Glebe land belonging to the Church and was not supposed to be built on.

    The Vicar of St. Leonard's lived at 115 Middleton Road, but about 1934 the Church built a fine new vicarage on the corner, next to the Church. No expense was spared and it was built to, the then, latest modern design. Later two police houses and a police office were built on the other corner. During the War a temporary building was put up as a Day Nursery for young children whose mothers were doing War Work. For a time after the War it was an Infants School and then modernised and is now a Nursery School. The meadow has since gone and the area is now occupied by sheltered housing.

IV Neighbours

Our neighbours when we first moved to 107 Middleton Road were old Mrs Painter, her daughter Miss Painter and their housekeeper/companion. Their house, 109 Middleton Road, had always been kept in excellent condition and not allowed to get shabby and run down as ours had, but their garden was small and not as pretty. For years Miss Painter had nursed and cared for her mother, until in 1939 the old lady died and Miss Painter gave up the house and moved to the country.

The house was then rented out to a Mrs Pearl Lord and her two little children. They had been living in Malta where Pearl's husband Bill was stationed as an engineer in the Navy. When the War broke out in 1939 all Navy wives and children were hastily and with great secrecy evacuated to England.

Pearl and her children had a terrible journey home. First there was a long wait for their ship to get a place in the convoy, then the convoy was attacked and several ships sunk. The ship was crowded with women and children and at night, below decks, it was airless and unbearably hot as all the portholes had to be kept tightly closed because of the strict blackout. Finally on arriving home they went straight to Pearl's mother, Mrs Cummings, who lived in Portsmouth. Because of strict censorship and secrecy about shipping movements, no one knew about the evacuation from Malta, so when Mrs Cummings opened the door and found them so unexpectedly standing there, she just greeted them by saying, 'you might have let me know you were coming!' She had no idea what they had been through.

For a while Pearl stayed with her mother but she wanted to get settled somewhere safer, as Portsmouth was a dangerous place because of air raids on the docks and naval yards. Bill's folks who were farmers at Middleton Cheney, heard of a house in Banbury that was empty and let Pearl know at once, as houses in safe areas were hard to come by. At first the solicitor was undecided if she could have the house but was finally persuaded as he was so charmed with her little boy, Brian. He agreed to rent the house to her for six months, giving her an option to buy. Soon after they moved in, Mrs Cummings' house was bombed, so she too came to Banbury. My mother got on famously with her new neighbours and became particularly fond of Pearl.

I was living in Old Grimsbury Road with my two girls and as Charles was stationed with the Army away from home, in 1941 I moved back to 107 Middleton Road with my parents. We had the big front bedroom on the first floor, my parents the bedroom at the back, whilst the evacuees had the other bedrooms. Old Grimsbury Road was let to other evacuees. It was a happy arrangement. The young Lords and our children were about the same age and they were soon good friends.

Pearl gave super Christmas and birthday parties for her children. Weeks before the event she would save up her rations and for two or three days before the party was busy cooking and preparing the food. Several of her friends always came to help, serving the food and looking after the children. The boys always formed a rowdy gang, wrestling on the floor or racing round the garden along the top of the walls. My eldest daughter always joined the boys and usually led the race along the walls, while my second daughter enjoyed playing quietly with the other girls and the babies. Everyone, including the helpers, had a wonderful time, as it was nice to have some festivities to cheer us all up during the War years.

Bill seldom had any leave but it was jolly when he did as he was such a lively and friendly person, always busy doing jobs about the house and garden or talking to the neighbours. Bill's War years saw much action. He was serving with the warship *Warsprite* and was with her when she was bombed at Salerno in 1943. On transferring to the *Hurricane*, she was also bombed and he and the other engineers were in the engine room trying to start the engines when the ship went down. The men found themselves in the water. Bill was lucky to survive as most of his comrades drowned. He was in hospital for six months. As his health was affected he was given a shore job as an instructor at a training establishment until the end of the war. Bill and Pearl had two more children. The children were all good-looking and clever and Bill and Pearl were devoted parents. Their children and home were their whole life. At the time of writing these memoirs Mr and Mrs Lord still live at 109 and it has remained exactly the same.

The next house in the terrace of four was 111 Middleton Road. Here lived Mr and Mrs Bernard Smith and their grown-up son and daughter. Bernard Smith had a large drapery shop in Parsons Street, opposite another small shop where he sold beautiful lingerie, corsetry and children's and babies' clothes. His business was thriving and as his wife wanted a house in a more fashionable area, he moved and bought a fine large house in Hightown Road.

Mr Smith wanted to get rid of the old house quickly so he put a notice in the sitting room window offering it for sale for £600, which was very cheap as the house had a large modern kitchen built on the back, a double garage but even though it had a huge garden, about three times the size of 107's, it was very dull and uninteresting.

A few days after he had put the notice in the window, Mrs Eaton came into his shop. She plonked her handbag on the counter, announcing she had brought the money and wanted to buy the house. She was so disappointed when she found that she had to go to a solicitor and that legal documents had to be drawn up before she could own it.

Mr and Mrs Eaton had seven grown-up children – four girls, Olive, Myrtle, Pearl and Ruby – three boys, George, Algernon and Eric. The Eatons all looked alike. They were short, fair and nearly all of them had very curly hair. Mrs Eaton was a tiny stout person with very splay feet. She was friendly and good-hearted and the family were devoted to her, always speaking of her with pride as 'Our Mother'.

Mr Eaton was a butler and daughter Olive was a parlourmaid in a large house in London, so were only at home at holidays, while George, one of the boys, was in the army in India. The rest of the Eatons were employed at E.W. Brown's Original Cake Shop in Parsons Street. Algernon and Eric when they first left school were errand boys, then were promoted to bakehouse boys. Eric later sold Banbury Cakes on Banbury Station to the passengers as they passed through. Myrtle was a bakehouse assistant and waitress, while Pearl was head of the ladies bakehouse. They worked at Brown's for years and were noted for being very hard workers. Misses Brown and my father thought a great deal of all of them and were sorry when they left.

When the Eaton family moved to 111 Middleton Road it suited them perfectly. There was plenty of room for them all and when each of the girls got married, for a while, she and her husband would live in the house until they could afford a house of their own. It was a large and busy household. During the War the men did the garden and grew the vegetables, keeping a large flock of hens in the back garden, and a pig in the garage. When Pearl Eaton and her husband, Gerald Robbins lived at home, he had three or four hives of bees which produced very fine honey. The bees made a wonderful difference to the neighbouring gardens. We'd never had such lovely flowers and crops of fruit before. We sorely missed the bees when Gerald and Pearl moved to their own home and took their hives with them.

I remember how, every day, Mrs Eaton would go up town just before 11 am to meet a group of her friends at Bennett's Wine Shop in Parsons Street. The ladies always sat in the small room beside the shop where they all had their 'special places' and were annoyed if anyone intruded on them. Just before 2 pm the party would break up and the ladies would set off for their homes. A little while later Mrs Eaton's diminutive figure would be seen coming along Middleton Road. She appeared to be walking very fast but she was actually taking such tiny steps it was ages before she would eventually arrive home for dinner, which one of her family would cook.

None of the boys ever married, so when the girls had all left home there was just Mrs Eaton and her three sons left. Myrtle, who lived close by, came in every day to clean, while the boys kept house and looked after their mother as she was getting old and needed care. When she died she left the house to her sons for as long as they needed a home. The brothers however were not harmonious. One brother shut himself away in a separate part of the house and seldom saw or spoke to the other two, almost becoming a recluse. This situation had been going on for a long time, until one day the two brothers realised they had not heard him moving about or seen him for some days. His door was locked and when they had the door broken down they found him dead inside. He had been dead for about a week. It was a great shock for the family and the two remaining brothers moved out at once and went to live with their sisters. It was a sad end to the old home which is now converted to flats and belongs to a Housing Association.

V 'Pineapple chunks 3½d, pink salmon 6d'

I loved Grimsbury and lived there for almost 25 uninterrupted years except for time during the War and when I was first married. It was a community, like living in a very large village where everybody knew everybody and all about each other. A great many young people and some of the prettiest and smartest girls in Banbury lived in Grimsbury.

It was a very convenient place to live as, except for furniture and clothing, everything you needed could be bought there. The large number of general stores, some nothing more than someone's front room, sold an amazing variety of things. There were butchers, greengrocers, hairdressers, shoe-repairers, a Post Office, newsagent, coal merchants, garages, a chemist, several public houses, beer retailers, off-licences and four or five farms and dairies, who all delivered milk daily. The four bakers made and baked their own bread and cakes on their premises and then delivered them.

Most of the shopkeepers lived behind and above their shops and knew all their customers, so the shops were great places for a chat and exchanging the latest news. Except for a few bad payers, everyone had credit and a weekly order and popped in, or sent their children for anything else they needed during the week, settling up at the end of the week when the men had their wages.

This was a time before homes and shops had all the modern conveniences which are now so much taken for granted. There were no ordinary fridges, freezers, ready-packed or frozen food; only the butchers had cold stores, which were large walk-in refrigerators.

Food was bought as it was needed or picked fresh from your garden or purchased from someone's allotment. Only a few things like tea, sugar and flour came in packets. The bigger businesses bought whole sides of bacon, whole cooked hams and big cheeses weighing at least 14 lbs, which were all cut up and weighed while the customers waited. There was always a great variety of cheap tinned food. Luxuries like pineapple chunks for 3½d, pink salmon for 6d, tinned peas for 3d and large tins of tomatoes for 9d. Every week Lyons delivered to the shops their cakes which were very cheap and immensely popular. A sultana cake was 9d, jam tarts 1½d each, 4 cup cakes in a box for 3½d, a snow cake covered in marshmallow icing and coconut and cut into six pieces cost 9d. But the great favourites were their swiss rolls and sponge cakes.

Throughout these memoirs I have referred to pounds, shillings and pence, the 'old currency'. To assist readers to convert old money to present currency here is a brief table, but you will of course appreciate there has been a vast change in the value.

Old money		New Money
6d	equivalent	2½p
1/–	equivalent	5p
2/–	equivalent	10p
10/–	equivalent	50p

There were the shopkeepers and vans selling things and some of Banbury's best specialist craftsmen lived or ran their own businesses in Grimsbury. The fine French Polishers, Mr Prescott and his sons from Howard Road, were just one such firm. Mr Gilbert Adkins and his family lived in St. Leonard's House on the corner of West Street from where he ran a wholesale potato depot.

J. Adkins & Sons' Greengrocery van came round selling fresh fruit and the vegetables they had grown in their Grimsbury Nursery in Overthorpe Road. It was a lovely Nursery Garden and they sold a great variety of plants, shrubs and flowers. Mr George Crisp lived at 35 West Street and once a week he went round with his big old van which was like a travelling ironmongers. He sold all sorts of pots, pans, brushes, brooms, cleaning materials, paraffin, paraffin stoves, china, rugs and sometimes even a carpet. Later Mr Hobbs bought the business and continued to run it in exactly the same way. Tuesdays and Fridays a man pushed round a barrow selling fish. The fish was laid out on the barrow with nothing covering it. There were some bits of newspaper for wrapping and a small spring balance for weighing. In spite of the dust and flies no one seemed to suffer any ill effects from eating it. Three nights a week in Winter, a van selling fish and chips toured around the streets. They did a very brisk trade for as soon as people smelt the frying fish and chips, they came hurrying out of their houses to buy their suppers. The fish and chips were fried on a stove in the van which had a chimney billowing out smoke. Sometimes the stove caught alight and set the van on fire.

This was just a taste of a few of the many splendid foods you could buy. Food was cheap and plentiful but times were hard and most people had very little money to spend.

Today that food may seem very uninteresting. No 'Big-Macs' or exotic flavours of 'E' numbers. But food was fresh and wholesome. After all in the 1950s chicken was a special treat, not an everyday meal.

3. *St Leonards School, Middleton Road.*

VI *'Chopin with silk ties'*

Down the garden path of 107 Middleton Road and through the back gate, was the short cut that my father took to take him to the Methodist Chapel and Sunday School Room in West Street. In the old days, the big West Street Methodist Chapel was packed out every Sunday. In the Sunday School room, a large Sunday School was held in the mornings, in the afternoons an Adult School, while during the week all sorts of meetings and social clubs, including the Methodist Band rehearsals. As well as the Chapel there was also a large elementary school.

Walter Timms, the builder, was the prime mover in keeping the Adult School going and he contributed generously to all its expenses. Only about a dozen came to the Adult School, but they all enjoyed it, taking turn to offer opening and closing prayers and leading the discussions. The pianist for the Chapel was a Miss Mellors, a little cripple woman, who had to have a taxi from her school in Marlborough Road, to bring her and her friend to the Meeting. People felt sorry for Miss Mellors as she was a cripple but didn't like her much. Her school didn't pay well so she was usually in financial difficulties but Walter Timms was wonderfully generous to her and often got her out of debt. He had the reputation of being mean and a hard businessman but really he was a most generous person and my parents thought a lot of him. When they moved to our home in West Bar and my mother was dying of cancer, Walter visited her regularly and every Sunday afternoon came and fetched my father so that he could still attend the Adult School in West Street.

Gradually attendances dropped at the Chapel, until there were only a handful of the faithful left. Sadly that old building has now been pulled down and a modern purpose-built edifice has replaced it, along with the character and charm. I remember when the building was being demolished, a neighbour in West Bar was so excited to be able to buy hand-made Victorian bricks from the demolition site to pave her patio. She had scoured the country to find them to try to restore her house with the same type of brick. There seems to be something very wrong when one side of Banbury is destroyed while the other end is trying to restore and be sensitive to architecture and preservation.

On the same side as the Methodist Chapel lived Walter South, the music teacher. He lived in a tall house with an imposing frontage. A flight of steps led up to the front door. The sitting room where he gave his music lessons had a bay window which overlooked the street below. Most years Walter had the outside of his house painted in an unusual colour scheme. One year it was a bright mauve front door and windows, all picked out with white with new mauve curtains and white nets to match. For every change of colour scheme he had new curtains to tone with the paintwork. As most people had their houses painted dark brown and cream and expected their paintwork to last a long time, everyone waited with great interest to see what Walter's outlandish new colour scheme would be.

Walter was short-sighted, very tall and thin with crooked shoulders, long thin hands and feet, a mincing walk and a face a little like 'Mr Punch's'. He wore an expensive camel hair coat with a belt and turned up collar, an expensive fur felt slouch hat, huge gauntlet gloves and very flashy silk ties and scarves. Unkind people said he 'liked the boys'. Walter was a very good but flamboyant pianist, loving to play Chopin, usually with his windows wide open so the

4. *St Leonards Parish Church, Middleton Road.*

5. *The Methodist Church and School Room, Marlborough Road.*

music could be heard up and down the street. He was an excellent music teacher and had a long waiting list of people wanting to have lessons. His beautiful grand piano was his pride and joy and with great self-sacrifice he let his pupils use it for their lessons. When he was pleased with a pupil's progress he gave them one of his old silk ties or scarves as a reward.

He lived with, and supported his mother in comfort, a brother he didn't get on with and his two sisters. His brother had a second-hand bookshop in 'Tink-a-Tank' by St. Mary's Church but seldom worked as he had nervous trouble, as a result of his War Work, in the Friends Ambulance Unit during the 1914-18 War. His older sister kept house for them all and together she and Walter cared for and nursed, first their mother and later their poor little crippled sister, who could barely walk. Walter was devoted to her and used to carry her carefully about the house and up and down the front steps to her invalid chair when she was taken for a walk. He was a lonely man with few friends. Although he was so peculiar, he was gentle and charming and while people laughed at him behind his back, they respected him for his kindness to his family and for his music.

West Street was no different from the other streets in Grimsbury. People not only lived in the houses but ran small business from their front rooms. Two houses down from Walter South's, was Mr and Mrs Eels' greengrocery and general shop. Mrs Eels was a stout woman with a florid complexion, Mr Eels thin and dark with a big nose and a drooping moustache. Mr Eels grew most of the vegetables for the shop on his allotments and also went around selling them from a handcart. The shop was a great place to gather for a chat, exchange gossip, listen to the music coming from Walter's house and make remarks about his newest colour scheme and neckties.

Further down West Street, two doors down from the Methodist Chapel, was Mr and Mrs Mather's house with its grocery and butchers shop. The shop was clean and neat and they sold good meat and bacon and a great variety of good class grocery. They did a brisk trade but although the Mathers were polite and friendly their shop was not a place to stay for a chat or hear the latest gossip.

After that there was only a beer retailer, before you came to Mrs Twynham's general shop at the bottom of West Street. It was a tiny place in the front room of her little house but it was crammed with stock. Patent remedies, sweets, cigarettes, cakes, tinned goods, firelighters, mousetraps, you name it and she stocked it. There was always a whole cooked ham, a tongue, a big piece of corned beef, two 14 lb red and white big round cheeses standing on the counter and a half side of bacon hanging at the back of the shop. Mrs Twynham cut off what you wanted while you waited. She was a large friendly woman who must have been very good-looking in her youth but I don't think she was popular with her neighbours, and customers as although her shop was always busy, no one stayed to talk.

On the opposite side of West Street and on the corner of North Street, was an off-licence called 'Our House', which was kept by a Mr Jarvis, who was Doctor Dwyer's chauffeur. Mrs Jarvis bred beautiful pedigree Cairn Terriers which were much sought after and the envy of all the dog fanciers. She exercised them four times a day and used to emerge from her front door surrounded by a crowd of six or seven little dogs on leashes, all barking their heads off with joy to be going for their walk. For several years after Mr Jarvis died, Mrs Jarvis carried on the business by herself until the War, when she was forced to close because of the shortage of liquor.

6. Stroud's Farm, 'Mild May', Banbury Lane, (Middleton Road).

VII Bull's Milk

West Street came to an abrupt end with a five-bar gate leading to a meadow. On the left-hand side, in 1937, Fergusson Road estate was built (initially called West Street Estate). On the right-hand side were Gibbs Road, Old Grimsbury Road, Old Grimsbury and Grimsbury Green leading onto the old Daventry Road.

In 1935 I married Charles Lester and from 1936 to 1940 we lived in one of the first modern houses to be built in Old Grimsbury Road. There was a row of eleven and ours was the third. It was the end of the town with pleasant country lanes, hedges and fields. Even so we were not cut off from the rest of the town. Every twenty minutes buses ran from Grimsbury Green up to the Town Hall, with another bus back again. There was a special bus laid on to collect Aluminium workers to take them to their shifts and bring them away. The shifts were; six in the morning until two in the afternoon, two in the afternoon until ten in the evening, ten in the evening until six in the morning.

One drawback to the scenery was the fact that the railway marshalling yards were nearby. Night and day we could see the work going on and hear the continual noises of the shunting. We got so used to the noise that we found Sundays eerily quiet when the yard was closed. But sharp on midnight everything started up again with a great clatter and bang and the floodlights mounted on full standards, would fill the place with light.

The eleven modern houses in old Grimsbury Road were built in a corner of a beautiful meadow, where a Mrs Bull grazed her herd of pedigree Jersey cows. Mrs Bull's Dairy sold 'luxury' milk and Mr Bull, as a concession, would deliver it to a few chosen customers, carrying it round in two large milk cans hanging from the crossbar of his bicycle. Of course, there were many rude jokes made about 'Bull's milk!'

Next to the Bulls was a row of little cottages with long gardens in front. They were poor primitive places, just two up and two down with a lean-to kitchen and outside toilet at the back. They belonged to Mr Bonham who lived in Boxhedge, on the other side of town.

One day there was a terrible rainstorm which flooded the meadow and our gardens. The water came almost over the top of our back doorsteps and into our kitchens. The road was flooded and the water rushed over the road into Mr Bonham's cottages, which were slightly lower than the road – the poor tenants having to take refuge in their upstairs rooms. Council men came at once to investigate. They found the big land drain at the bottom of Old Grimsbury Road and the meadow, behind our houses, had formerly discharged its matter onto the land on which the new houses in Fergusson Road stood and when the houses were built, instead of putting in new drains, the old drain had simply been blocked up! There was a great fuss over who was to blame. Eventually the council put in new drains and the builders paid a proportion of the cost.

Mr Molyneaux's Bakehouse and Baker's shop was always popular for its good bread and nice cakes – it was a thriving business. Mrs Molyneaux and their youngest daughter, Marjorie, looked after the shop. Mr and Mrs Molyneaux were always having fierce arguments, usually while she was serving and he was standing in the doorway of the bakehouse. It was disconcerting for the customers who found their arguments embarrassing. Marjorie tried to keep the peace as she loved both her parents. In spite of their differences Mr and Mrs Molyneaux were united in their love and devotion to her and the rest of their children. She was a sweet girl, liked by everyone, but sadly she had a badly curved spine and was very delicate.

We were lucky enough at this time to have a car. Charles had been given an MG sports car by his father for a 21st birthday present. My parents also had a car, an Austin Seven. We both belonged to the RAC and both bought our petrol at the County Garage by Banbury Cross as it was so much cheaper than anyone else's.

The RAC man was a Mr Franklyn. I think RAC men were known as 'Scouts'. Every day he would be employed to stand at Banbury Cross, saluting every motorist whose car bore an RAC badge. I remember how pleased everyone was at this 'service' and how chuffed. When the service was discontinued there was a great outcry. Mr Franklyn apart from saluting all cars was employed to attend to any breakdowns and repairs. He didn't have a car though, just a bicycle with a tool box on the back and you had to wait until he pedalled along to repair your car. Times have certainly changed.

Opposite our house there were five older type houses. Mr and Mrs Sewell and their daughters lived in the first one. Its front door was in Gibbs Road, number 22. Mr and Mrs Grant and their son Alfie lived in the second. Mr Grant was a railwayman and Alfie a hairdresser. Everyone knew Alfie as for years he was pianist in Ken Prewer's Dance Band. During the War he was in the Royal Corps of Signals and spent a long time in Egypt. After the War he teamed up again with Ken Prewer, until in 1956 when Brownie Lay broke away forming his own dance band.

In the fourth house lived Mr and Mrs Day and their family of five – four girls and a boy. Mr Day was a quiet man. He worked on the railway and spent most of his free time on his allotment. Mrs Day was a cheerful, pretty little person. She sold a few cigarettes, sweets and one or two groceries from her front room and there was a constant stream of neighbours dropping in for a chat or occasionally to buy something. The shop was convenient for us, as we could pop across the road if we wanted cigarettes or sweets, during an evening. The Days' children were charming, especially the third girl, Doris. She had a mop of curly auburn hair and was bright and friendly. She was her mother's 'right-hand man', doing odd jobs, running errands and looking after the baby and her little brother when she wasn't at school. My little girls loved her and she used to come with her girl friend and take them and her baby brother and sister for walks.

Mrs Day kept a large mangle standing outside her side door and one or two galvanized wash tubs hanging on the wall. Wash-day was a day of great activity in the Day household with Mrs Day working very hard washing and then mangling the clothes, standing outside the side door.

In those days there were no washing machines or spin driers. Everything had to be washed and wrung out by hand or mangled if you were lucky enough to have a mangle. The newer houses had gas boilers for heating the water and boiling the clothes, which made washing a little easier. Older houses had a big stand built of bricks in a corner of the back kitchen to hold a large, deep, galvanized or copper bowl, with a heavy wooden lid. Underneath was a place for a fire and a brick chimney with a flue going out through the roof.

Early Monday morning the copper had to be filled with water and a fire lighted under it to heat the water. White things like sheets and table-cloths were put in to boil first. When they had boiled, the hot steaming laundry was lugged out with a wooden stick and a pair of large wooden tongs, rinsed in a large washtub, dipped in another rinse of 'Reckitts Blue', mangled and hung out to dry. Things like table-cloths and men's collars had to be starched, usually in a bowl of Robin's starch which was made up in advance. Next the coloured things were washed and lastly all the dirty things, like men's working overalls. Very heavy things needed two people to handle them. When the washing was finished the kitchen floor was washed with the remains of the hot water, the copper and all the tubs cleaned and dried. As well as being hard work the old way of boiling and lugging about heavy loads of steaming hot clothes and having tubs of hot water standing on the floor was dangerous. There were some terrible accidents from scalding, especially to young children.

There was nothing like our modern detergents and soap powders, only soda, yellow soap and soft soap, ammonia, borax, ACDO tablets and Rinso and Lux soap-flakes. The only gadgets to help were a wash-board to rub the clothes on and a dolly stick to swish them about. On wash-day the whole house smelt of the boiling clothes and the doors and windows had to be kept open because of the steam. In wet weather there were lines of damp washing hanging up in the kitchen or drying in front of the fire.

When the washing was dry enough, it was ironed on the kitchen table with a flat iron. The irons were heated in front of the kitchen fire or on a gas ring. They got very hot and the handles had to be held with a thick pad and the iron rubbed clean, usually on the mat. To test if the iron was hot, you spat on the face of it and if the spit sizzled up and rolled off, the iron was hot enough. When electric irons were invented they were a great improvement but they were quite dangerous as few people had power points and just a ceiling light. They would plug the iron into the electric light fitting by means of a long dangling flex. The flex would often be pulled so taut that part of the ceiling would come down with the electrical fitting! The ceiling light was not meant to be used for domestic appliances and it would fuse with the overloading of the circuit. Many people didn't understand that the irons were thermostatically controlled and still tested them by spitting.

Larger houses had a proper wash-house built at the back of the house and a woman was employed to come in for the day to do the washing or if it could be afforded the washing was sent out to a laundry who collected it in your personal wicker hamper and brought it back at the end of the week. The laundries however used such harsh chemicals that the clothes wore out quickly. If you couldn't afford to send to a laundry or have a woman come in for the day, there was always some poor soul with children or an unemployed husband to support, who was glad to do your washing in her own home for just a few shillings. She usually did washing for several other families as well. Her children helped by collecting the dirty washing, helping with the mangling and delivering the washing back when it was clean. If they were lucky you gave them 2d!

Many women took great pride in having snowy white washing. Personally I hated washing. My washing was a dingy shade of grey. I had quantities to do and it was even worse when we had four children, no mangle and couldn't afford to send it to the laundry, so imagine my joy when my husband bought me a washing machine just before our fifth child was born. It was a wonderful machine and saved hours of drudgery. My mother never had or wanted a washing machine but then she always managed to find someone else to do her washing or sent it to the laundry.

After the Day's house and the eleven new houses, there was nothing until you came to a row of thatched stone cottages which faced down Old Grimsbury Road. They looked very picturesque with large cottage gardens and an old well in front of them. Inside however, they were dreadful places – small, pokey, with earth floors and no modern conveniences – but the rent was only a few shillings a week. They belonged to Henry Sommerton who came from an old Warwickshire family of millers (he was a relation of my husband). He was well off but he was a miser. Although he owned a lot of property and earned good money doing shift work at the 'Ally' (the Aluminium Works) he lived in an old trailer and did odd gardening jobs and hair cutting. Then there was a row of brick cottages also with long front gardens.

A Mr and Mrs Baldwin lived in one of the cottages. Mr Baldwin, who was deranged and an invalid, as a result of the Great War, needed constant attention and watching. To help support them, Mrs Baldwin had a tiny shop in the front room, where she sold cigarettes, cheap sweets and a little tinned food. She was a smart woman, and always wore make-up and bright coloured fashionable clothes. But she had a hard life and it was a struggle for her to make both ends meet. Her house was famous for her garden which was full of garden gnomes. Everyone would stop and laugh at the quantity of gnomes.

Opposite the cottages was the entrance to Grimsbury Manor. The Manor was up a long drive surrounded by beautiful wooded grounds and in Spring, masses of snowdrops and daffodils grew either side of the drive under the trees. Mr Lamley Fisher, who was a Solicitor, Commissioner for Oaths and Registrar for Banbury and District, holding several other official posts, lived there with his wife. It was a beautiful home and the house and grounds were kept in perfect order. They entertained a great deal and in Summer held garden parties in the lovely grounds.

Mrs Lamley Fisher did a great deal of work for charities and always lent her house and garden for meetings and bazaars. She was especially interested in the Bluebird League of Pity (a children's charity) and the RSPCA, encouraging children to take an interest in the work and to have collecting boxes. The children looked forward to and enjoyed the box opening ceremonies at the Manor, when certificates were handed out saying how much had been collected. Every Winter she organised a Children's Fancy Dress Ball in aid of the charities, which was held in the Church House. They were always packed with children in all sorts of Fancy Dress and at the end there was a grand parade around the room when the judges decided which were the best costumes.

When the Lamley Fishers moved from Grimsbury to a smaller house in the more fashionable area of West Bar, the big house started to become run down. Subsequent owners found it too expensive to keep up the repairs and the value of the property dropped especially after the enlargement of the railway and finally the building of the cold store right on its boundaries.

In the late 1950s being now owned by a man nicknamed 'Holy Joe' part of the Manor was turned into flats and let to American servicemen and their families. The flats weren't at all convenient but the Americans loved the large rooms and beautiful grounds.

Holy Joe sold tomatoes, cucumbers, lettuces and vegetables which he grew in the old greenhouses and vegetable garden and would prop up a board by the entrance gates to say what was for sale. I often bought his vegetables as they were very good and I enjoyed the walk to the Manor, up the drive to the kitchen, where he sold them. The part of the lane that passed the Manor has now disappeared to make way for the new road and industrial units. The big stone house stands alone and derelict beside Hennef Way.

Continuing past the Manor, the lane crossed the old brick railway bridge, where we used to stop to watch the passing trains, then on to 'Field's Mill'. There had been a water mill and until recently the water wheel was intact and in working order. It was called Field's Mill as it belonged to a Mr Field who lived in the house beside the mill. Before it was altered it was a fine house with a bay window overlooking the lane and the small stone bridge which crossed the river. In wet weather the water rushed under the bridge and often flooded the surrounding meadows and the lane. The lane finished at a five-bar gate which was always kept closed, beyond which was the private road to the Waterworks and Waterworks House.

The private road was narrow and perfectly straight and crossed the meadows to another gate and the small drawbridge over the canal and on to the Southam Road. There were wire fences either side and it was raised about 3 ft above the meadows so that it wouldn't be flooded. It was just wide enough for a horse and cart and if anything came the other way one of them had to wait in one of the lay-bys. Very little passed along it, the occasional vehicle to the Waterworks, a man cycling to work or a few people taking a walk.

The Waterworks and Waterworks House had been built by the private company formed by James Cadbury and his friends when the town council had no money to provide a proper water supply for the town. The Waterworks used to be a plain red brick building with a chimney. As you passed you could hear the pumps chugging away inside and occasionally the chimney gave off bursts of steam. When the old pump was replaced it was so well fitted it was almost impossible to get out and in spite of its age showed no signs of wear.

The small quiet lane was our favourite walk until cars started to use it as a short cut to Southam Road when the traffic in the town became so congested. This led to endless trouble as the lane was never intended for quantities of traffic and the drawbridge was not strong enough for the procession of heavy cars. Long queues of cars formed when the drawbridge was opened for barges to pass through. It was a nightmare. The traffic going to and from work had ruined our pleasant country walk. The area is now totally unrecognisable. The meadows drained, with fast roads, bypasses and traffic islands taking their place.

VIII 'Oh Valiant Heart'

Harry Stroud junior, his wife Martha and their three little girls lived at Wildmere Farm, a brick house, in the same lane as Grimsbury Manor, but by Grimsbury Green. His father, Harry senior, owner of Wildmere and Mild May farms, had owned the butcher's shop in Middleton Road, which his son Bill had taken over. On retirement Harry senior had moved to Mild May and his second son Harry junior, after the 1914 War, had been set up by his father and lived in Wildmere with his new wife.

Harry had a very distinguished War record and served as a sergeant in the Queen's Own Oxfordshire Hussars from August 4th 1914 until March 1918 when he was badly wounded at the Battle of St. Quentin. He fought in all the major battles of the War and held the Mons Star. He kept wonderful diaries of the War, full of interesting anecdotes, which paint a vivid picture of the soldiers' lives and the conditions they lived through. Excerpts from his diaries and several mentions of him are quoted in the book 'The Queen's Own Oxfordshire Hussars'.

When he was wounded in the leg he suffered terribly. His comrades who were helping him, half dragged him along for 1½ miles, until they came across an old bedspring which they used as a stretcher to carry him on. When they reached the out-post there were no facilities to treat him so he had to endure a long ambulance ride over rough roads to a primitive hospital where his leg was amputated. It was done badly and the leg bone was left protruding. His first artificial leg was a wooden 'peg-leg' which he hated. He was invalided out and was sent to Uffculme Hospital, Edgbaston, Birmingham. It was here that Harry met my father and mother, Robert and Olive Pursaill. In 1914, my father, a conscientious objector had joined the Friends Ambulance Unit and was sent to France. He suffered shell-shock and was invalided home. When he had recovered, as he and my mother had worked for the Quakers doing social and welfare work, they took jobs at Uffculme.

Uffculme was a small private hospital in beautiful grounds and was financed by the Quaker, Barrow Cadbury, of the Bourneville chocolate factory and run by his wife, Geraldine Cadbury. The male staff were members of the Friends Ambulance Unit and were volunteers, the nurses young Quakeresses, VADS. A few dedicated and highly qualified doctors and nurses were in charge. It was an unpretentious place and the atmosphere was informal and friendly. They were doing pioneering work in the design and fitting of artificial limbs and the rehabilitation of patients. The methods they used were new and modern, even by today's standards.

My father, a member of the FAU, was quartermaster. He taught woodwork, toy making and various handicrafts to the patients and helped in teaching the patients to learn to walk and use their artificial hands and arms. He helped Harry learn to walk with his new artificial leg. He was my father's favourite patient. Every afternoon my mother and I visited the hospital and although I was only four, I remember how fond I was of Sergeant Harry and how kind he was to me. Everyone liked and respected him because of his cheerful bravery and the way he helped and cared for the other men.

As my father was a good athlete and before the War had helped to run a Quaker Social Club for men and boys in the East End of London, he helped with physical exercises and games for the patients. Sometimes there were sports days for them. These were happy occasions with crowds of visitors coming to watch and cheer, as the patients competed in all sorts of races, tugs of war and games of rounders. My mother and most of the spectators were very moved by the men's cheerfulness and courage as they struggled to compete in spite of their disabilities but were careful not to show any sign of emotion or pity. I remember one man who had lost both legs propelling himself along with his arms as he enthusiastically competed in a game of rounders. After the sports everyone stayed to talk and have tea.

The men were allowed to go out on Saturday nights but were asked not to drink beer as it was bad for their wounds. In spite of that most of them did! While the men were together in hospital they helped each other to keep cheerful and hopeful. But sadly when they got home they often became depressed and lonely and their families didn't understand or couldn't cope with their problems.

About 1919 Mr and Mrs Cadbury gave Uffculme to the City of Birmingham, who used it as a hospital for the treatment of shell-shock victims. As my father had no qualifications he was out of a job. He came to Banbury for an interview for a manager with the Misses Brown, Quakeresses, of the Original Cake Shop, who were offering work to unemployed Quakers. When he arrived at the station the first person he met was Harry Stroud. My father was delighted and looked on it as a good omen.

Gradually Harry settled down to a quiet life farming at Wildmere but he continued to suffer great pain from his old injury. In spite of that, he managed to live a normal life. He walked well, worked on his farm, drove a car and even danced at Masonic Ladies Nights.

When Harry died suddenly in April 1931 the town was stunned. He was buried with full Military Honours. The funeral was a tremendous affair and must have been the biggest the town has ever seen. All the way from Grimsbury to St. Mary's Church the streets were lined with people, many of them crying. The British Legion Band led the funeral procession playing 'Oh Valiant Hearts' and 'Abide With Me'. They were followed by 60 Officers and Men of the Queen's Own Oxfordshire Hussars, a large contingent of the Oxfordshire Yeomanry, about 40 Officers and Men of the Banbury Branch of the British Legion and large numbers from the branches in the surrounding county, and representatives from the 400th Battery of the Royal Artillery. They all wore red poppies and carried rolled and draped flags. Outside St. Mary's there was a Guard of Honour of the Oxfordshire Yeomanry and the British Legion. The coffin, draped with the Union Jack, was carried by bearers with old comrades walking either side. It was met at the Church gates by Canon Jones and led into the packed Church by the full choir following the Cross Bearer. As the entourage filed into the Church the organ played 'I know that My Redeemer Liveth' and Chopin's Funeral March. After the service the great procession moved on to the cemetery, led by the band playing the 'Funeral March in Saul'. Once again crowds were lining the route and the cemetery was thronged with mourners.

As the coffin was lowered into the grave the band played one verse of 'Oh Valiant Hearts' and then the Buglers sounded the Last Post. On the plain coffin the inscription read: 'Harry Stroud, died April 2nd 1931, aged 45'. Although the War was ended it continued to claim its victims.

After Harry's death Martha and her three little girls moved to a house in Middleton Road and Harry's cousin, Bib Stroud, took on the farm.

IX Butchers, Doctors, Undertakers

Over the canal bridge and over the railway bridge is the beginning of Middleton Road. On the left-hand side is a row of tall brick houses, Annie Southam's drugstore, where she sold every kind of patent medicine you could think of. Further on stood Strouds' butchers shop. The Strouds are a local family (I spoke of Harry in the previous chapter) and they were successful cattle dealers and farmers – some over in Overthorpe, Nethercote and Grimsbury. The Strouds' butchers shop had been passed from father to son – Harry to Bill. It was a large thriving business employing several men.

They did their own slaughtering in the yard behind the shop and the entrails and other waste was thrown into a big pit which was cleaned out when it was full or smelt too bad. They sold top grade meat and served customers all over the town. The customers' orders were delivered by smart little green pony traps pulled by sprightly ponies. The ponies were kept in the field behind the Methodist Chapel in West Street. Bill Stroud's wife Emily kept the books, did the accounts and sat in the cash desk at the back of the shop taking the money. There was no heating in the shop and the door was always kept wide open in summer and winter. In winter it was freezing cold in the shop and Emily wore woollen mittens to try to keep her hands warm as they got so red and swollen with the cold.

Everything was very clean. There was fresh sawdust on the floor, a big scrubbed pine counter and on the wall behind, a wide shelf to cut the meat on, with an assortment of knives, saws and choppers, with above, a row of big carcasses of meat hanging from shining brass hooks. In the window, the meat was displayed on a white marble slab or hung from a wide brass rod.

Bill Stroud was a short thick-set man with a round red face and Emily was medium height, very upright without an ounce of fat on her. She was very pale and wore her fair hair drawn back in a tight little bun. They both wore glasses. They loved dancing and went to all the local dances, and when they were young had won many dancing contests and prizes. They attended all the Masonic Ladies Nights, where Emily, who was tired and not used to the heat and rich food, used to fall asleep during the speeches, sitting bolt upright in her chair.

They were both immensely proud of their son and daughter, Harry and Evelyn. Harry held a prominent position at the Spencer Corset Factory and was a great favourite of the owners, Mr and Mrs Allen and a frequent visitor to their home in Sutton-under-Brailes. Harry eventually left Spencers, and with Bill and Emily's help, started his own business designing and manufacturing corsets and luxury lingerie somewhere in the North. Evelyn stayed at home and when she married they gave her a big wedding and reception and in the evening held a large dance at the Crown Hotel with a beautiful buffet and lots of drink. They also bought her a nice modern house in Bath Road and when they retired, went and lived opposite her, selling the butcher's business to Billy Kearse, who had worked for them for years.

29 Middleton Road, in the converted front room, was the Post Office run by Dorothy Barnes. The pillar box stood

in the front garden. Dorothy had been a supervisor at the General Post Office and was a charming, good-looking young woman liked by everyone. Her husband had a newspaper delivery business which he ran from a corner of the Post Office, but he seemed to do very little but sit in the room behind the office, shouting out orders and rude remarks to his wife. He was a very bad tempered man and I'm sorry to say that I don't think any of his customers or neighbours were sorry when he died suddenly when he was quite young. His wife managed very well without him and continued to run the Post Office and his newspaper business in her usual efficient manner.

A few doors down is the Cricketers pub. It hasn't really altered but the land behind it is quite different. At one time it was the sports ground for the old County School, but later, a Railway Hostel was built on it for the young railwaymen. The young railwaymen never liked the hostel even though there were games rooms and showers and a good canteen. It wasn't homely and they were much happier in lodgings, able to sit by a fire, drink cups of tea and chat with the family. When the hostel closed it was bought and run as a very peculiar hotel, which was pulled down in the 1980s and a block of flats built in its place.

Opposite the Cricketers, by the Bell and Mumford's garage lived Mr and Mrs McKeevor and their daughter Mary, in the big house which is now Hinkins and Frewins offices. Mr McKeevor had a rag and scrap metal business in the yard behind the house and Mary, a trained hairdresser, had a nice hairdressing salon in the two front bedrooms, employing two assistants. Mrs McKeevor did some of the perming, acted as receptionist and if the rations permitted, dished out cups of tea for the customers. They were always busy. I was a regular customer and enjoyed going there as it was such a clean and friendly place.

Next there were one or two small houses, then a row of eight brick cottages with long front gardens. They were poor hovels, just two up and two down with outside toilets in the small yards at the rear.

After this row of cottages was a turning to the right to Duke Street. It was only a rough little road and on the left ran past a barber's shop, owned by Alfie Grant, and past a disused brickyard which later Baldwin and Herbert used for their agricultural engineering business to a piece of spare ground which was used as a tip by the neighbourhood. Every kind of rubbish was dumped there. Parts of old bicycles, iron bed-ends, old cookers and hosts of other things people had thrown away. It was a wonderful place for the children, as they liked to climb about on the rubbish or sort through it looking for treasures.

Opposite the tip area was a row of thirty identical little brick houses. They all had exactly the same doorknobs, little letterboxes with fancy cast iron door knockers, no front gardens with the front doors opening directly into the small parlour room, behind which was the kitchen/living room. A door in the corner of the room opened directly onto the stair to the two bedrooms above.

At the back, a communal path ran behind all the houses and as the path passed directly by the kitchen windows you had to be careful not to pry in as you went by. Everybody had a tin bath hanging outside the back door and at the bottom of each of the small gardens were the toilets. There were no modern conveniences and very little privacy, everyone knowing each others affairs, but it was a community and people were very happy living there. Some people

7. *RAC Scout Mr Franklin at Banbury Cross.*

lived there for most of their lives and were sorry when the houses were demolished and they were moved to larger modern houses.

Carrying on up Middleton Road past St. Leonard's and 107 Middleton Road, on the left, was Doctor Dwyer and his wife who lived at 143 Middleton Road. It was a huge house in which was incorporated a tiny surgery and dispensary. The Dwyers employed a cook, a housemaid, a woman for the washing and rough work, a gardener and chauffeur. Before the acquisition of the car and chauffeur, Doctor Dwyer visited his patients on a bicycle.

An Irishman by birth, Doctor Dwyer was tall and thin with a gruff austere manner – but could be very charming and was well-liked and respected – indeed an old-fashioned family doctor. His full name was Hubert de Burgh Dwyer and he came from an aristocratic family in Ireland. His wife was a keen sportswoman, an excellent tennis player, a good musician and pianist and played the organ at St. Leonard's Church.

The Doctor and his wife were very proud of their three sons, who were strikingly good-looking young men with golden hair and pink and white complexions. They often came to visit their parents, driving dashing little sports cars and wearing sporty modern clothes. Gossip said that for many years the doctor had a lady-love and certainly there was another young man in town who bore a remarkable resemblance to the Dwyer boys.

Doctor Dwyer was doctor to most of Grimsbury. He charged 2/6d a visit, which included a bottle of medicine but you had to provide your own bottle or it was 2d extra. He bought large quantities of one or two sorts of ready made patent medicines and filled up your bottle with what he thought was appropriate for your ailment.

During surgery hours Dwyer's surgery was crowded with 'Panel Patients', the Government's National Insurance Scheme for workers, run by the insurance companies. The contribution for men was about 6d a week, women paying less. Everyone was provided with a registration number and a card which had to have an insurance stamp stuck on each week.

You chose your own Insurance Company and joined the Panel of the Doctor of your choice, becoming a 'Panel Patient'. The Temperance Insurance Companies offered much better benefits but only accepted bonafide teetotallers. If you fell ill and needed to claim, the rules for drawing 'Sick Pay' were very strict. You had to be home before 8 pm and could not leave the town without a very good reason and being granted special permission. As the scheme only covered the workers, not their dependants, most Doctors ran their own 'Sick Clubs' for the families. It cost about 3d a week and for a further 3d the 'Banbury Workpeople's Hospital Association' provided free hospital treatment and the cost of specialist fees for all the family.

As well as his general practice, Dwyer was the physician and surgeon for the 'Banbury Area Guardians Committee', – meaning he looked after the Workhouse inmates and was also the 'Certifying Factory Surgeon' and 'Medical Officer' and 'Public Vaccinator' for Banbury.

I was vaccinated by him in 1923 when there was a smallpox scare. For the vaccination your arm was punctured by four sharp little spikes attached to a small metal disc, then the vaccine was placed on the wounds and covered with a piece of lint. After seven days the arm became red and inflamed and very painful. Eventually scabs formed which

8. *The County Garage, 12 Horsefair.*

9. *Clark's Flour Mill, Station Road.*

took two or three weeks to dry and come off. As great care had to be taken not to knock the scabs, you wore a red arm band to warn people to be careful of your arm. The vaccination left four white scars each about the size of a new 5p coin which lasted the rest of your life. You still may see older people with these marks on their arms while the next generation has only one round scar on its arm. I think the present vaccination for smallpox leaves no mark at all.

Towards the end of Middleton Road and on the left in East Street there was a large firm of builders with a big timber yard and joinery shop – Grants. Grants were also undertakers and made the coffins in their joinery shop. Funerals were important occasions at which many customs were observed which have long since been discontinued and forgotten.

It is a comparatively modern idea to have a Chapel of Rest. In the old days the body was laid out in the sitting room or best bedroom, while relations, friends and neighbours called to pay their respects and see the body. All the curtains in the house were kept closed until after the funeral. It was dreadfully depressing, living in the gloomy half light and having the body in the house, especially as you were expected to stay at home and not go anywhere, except to work, until after the funeral.

At the funeral everyone would be dressed in black. The women relatives then wore black for at least six months and some widows were in black for several years. A few widows wore long black veils to cover their heads and faces when they went out, these were called 'Widow's Weeds'. For six months the men of the family wore black ties, black arm bands or diamonds of black cloth sewn on their coat sleeve.

To add to the gloom the Church funeral bell tolled at half-minute intervals, nine times for a man, six for a woman, three for a child and then one for each year of their lives, only stopping when the hearse and mourners reached the Church. As the procession left the house, everyone in the street closed their curtains and any passers-by stood on the kerb with bowed heads, the men with their hats off until it had passed slowly by. The undertaker walked in front of the hearse with the pall bearers walking either side of it, all of them wearing black top hats and black overcoats. After the funeral everyone was invited back to the house for a big tea and to meet relations, renew old friendships and make up old quarrels. Some old-fashioned families still had the Will read after the funeral. With all the black clothes, hushed voices, drawn blinds and the tolling bell, funerals were terrible occasions.

Grants, the builders, had once employed twenty men but the business had declined until there was only the son, John Grant and two men doing building repairs and the maintenance work. John was a reliable hard-working man and did a lot of repairs and decorating in Grimsbury. His work was good and he came at once when needed but he didn't make much money as he charged so little. He was a friendly man who everyone liked and it was a shock when he died suddenly. His death left his poor wife with their little boy to bring up and a building business to run. She coped very well but eventually sold everything, including some land opposite, where John had grown vegetables, to a developer who built houses and flats on it.

Right at the end of Middleton Road and at the corner of Daventry Road, on the left, is the Blacklock Arms. It was built in 1937 but never opened, just left standing empty. When the War started in 1939 it was requisitioned by the

10. *GWR Station, Station Approach.*

Army. The Liverpool Scottish was the first regiment billeted there. Several times a day the men marched up and down Middleton Road to their mess hall in the Blue Bird Hotel in Bridge Street. The sergeants had their mess at The Angel in the Market Place. It was a grand sight to see them in their tartan trews marching down the road led by their pipers. On special occasions they wore kilts. The men were popular with Grimsbury people and made a great many friends. Mr Mallaley, who belonged to the regiment married Miss Mold of Middleton Road. For the wedding he and the best man wore their kilts. After the War Mr Mallaley settled in Banbury and for many years was with the furnishing firm of Chapman Brothers.

Several other regiments were billeted at the Blacklocks but none of them were as popular as the Liverpool Scottish. After the War the place was refurbished and the pub opened.

After the Blacklock Arms, Middleton Road ends and what was known as Banbury Lane begins. Here Harry Stroud senior owned and lived in Mild May farm. One of Harry's daughters was Annie, who later married Horace Lester of 121 Middleton Road. I have painted the farmhouse with three of Harry's grandchildren, Joan, Horace and Ernest Lester, dressed in their sailor suits waving to their grandmother.

Mild May farmhouse was eventually sold, but not the land. The house was bought by a Mr Vaughan Smith for Dog Kennels. About 1937 Mrs Vaughan Smith built an open-air swimming bath and Lido beside the house. It was very popular as it was heated and floodlit until 10 pm every night. There was a pretty fountain, nice refreshments and changing rooms only costing 1/6d admittance. When the War started it was closed and requisitioned by the Army. Troops were billeted in the Lido buildings, and coal stored in the swimming bath. After the War the house had several owners and ended up as a scrap merchant's yard with a garage in front. Now the farmhouse and buildings have been pulled down and the site cleared for the new developments.

The other farm in the area was Manor Farm on the corner of Daventry Road and Grimsbury Green. It was William Webb's farm. He and his wife lived there with their only child, a very pretty girl called Flossy, whom they idolised. Once or twice my mother and I were invited to tea. Mrs Webb provided a lavish tea with home-made scones, jams and cakes, in their large flagstoned kitchen, while Mr Webb sat in an antique wooden armchair beside the big stone fireplace telling us about the old house and how it was reputed that Charles I stayed there.

Mr Webb and Mr Stroud were great friends, so both families were pleased when Flossy married Mr Stroud's youngest son Sidney. Flossy and Sidney went to live in South Street and managed Webb's Dairy. When they started bottling the milk they changed the name to the Model Dairy and opened a modern milk bar in the Market Place. Both businesses were very successful as Flossy had a good head for business.

On a map you can see how, at the beginning of Middleton Road, on the right is the Causeway, running nearly parallel and leading onto Overthorpe Road, with School View and Howard Road branching off, and joining up again at the top of Middleton Road and the Daventry Road.

Causeway has changed very little except the shabby little houses on the left have been pulled down. The new houses and apartments built in their place are a great improvement. It is still the friendly place it used to be, with neighbours dropping in for a chat, ready to help if there is trouble. There were four general shops, a butcher, coal merchant, hairdresser and an off-licence. Most people had large families and favourite places for the children to play were Spiceball Park, the rough ground at the end of Duke Street and the Meadow in Middleton Road. Larry Grayson had connections with the Causeway as did Gary Glitter for a time.

Causeway ended at a farm gate across what is now Overthorpe Road, beyond which was a footpath crossing the fields to Nethercote Lane. When the Munitions Factory was built in 1915, in what is now Overthorpe Road, the footpath was opened up so that the workers could get to work without having to go all the way round by Nethercote Lane.

School View was the last turn on the left of the Causeway and got its name from the Council School which was very modern and up-to-date when it was built in 1910. When the old Methodist School in West Street was closed, the pupils were transferred to this new school. Mr Stuchbury, who still lives in Causeway, was one of the first pupils and remembers leaving the old Methodist School and being marched round in a crocodile to the new school. In the old days most children received all their education at one school – starting when they were five and leaving when they were fourteen or if they were clever, winning a scholarship to the County School when they were eleven, where they stayed until they were sixteen or more.

Although the official age for starting school was five, many Council Schools had Infant Departments taking children from the age of three. Grimsbury Council School was one of them and had a particularly good Infants Department. The rooms had cheerful decorations and little chairs and tables for groups of children to work at. There was a lot of play time and a good selection of toys, some of them large and expensive. By the time the children were five they could read well, under the guidance of Miss Frances Thornton, Miss Cooper, a pupil teacher and headmaster Mr Scroxton. Those with reading problems had special tuition. Every afternoon the children got out little canvas beds and blankets, laid down for a rest and listened to the teacher reading a story. No one made a sound and most of the younger ones fell asleep.

X A Throne of White Flowers

Before the beginning of Middleton Road, Station Road branches off to the right at the top of Bridge Street over the canal bridge. It was privately owned. The road was blocked on Good Fridays by a rope, slung across and there was a man in charge, who unhooked the rope when people wanted to pass. It was done to prevent the road becoming a 'right of way'. To use it, the businesses in Station Road paid an annual rent. The road was very rough and full of pot holes and the carts and taxis bumped along it in an alarming manner. Visitors to the town wondered why we had such a fearful approach to the station.

Dalby's timber and builder's merchants yard, 1 Bridge Street, was on the right-hand corner of Bridge Street and Station Road, and belonged to Mr W.S. Orchard. At one time Dalby's was a large busy yard employing a great many men. As most of their stocks were delivered on the canal, they had a strange wooden structure built above and over the canal for unloading their goods from the barges. But as their trade declined, Dalby's became a shabby place, employing only a few men. The storage sheds were almost derelict and empty, except for piles of old stock. Eventually it was sold and is now modernized.

Halfway down Station Road, on the right-hand side was 'Clark's Mill'. It was a modern mill built in 1910 by Theo Clark and his father Thomas. Although no longer a mill, the building hasn't altered and you can still see 'Flour Mill' painted in big white letters at the top of the centre tower. The small building on the right of the Mill was the office, built well away from the main building so that office work was not disturbed by the noise and flour dust from the Mill. When the Mill was working, it made a great deal of noise and all around Station Road was a covering of a white dusting of flour.

It was a big mill supplying high grade flour to most of the leading biscuit manufacturers, such as Huntley and Palmers, Crawfords and Cadburys. The grain was brought by canal and unloaded by a large hoist and taken to the top of the Mill to be ground. When finished, the sacks of flour were collected by horse drawn wagons from the big door on the ground floor or loaded onto the canal barges. The flour originally had to be collected on a dry day for if it got wet it was spoilt. A large covered extension was later added to the front of the Mill so the flour could be collected no matter what the weather.

The owners, Mr and Mrs Theo Clark, and their four children, lived in a big house 'Rockholme', High Town Road. It was a private road full of ruts and holes, with a few big houses on the right side going down and a row of smaller houses on the left.

Mr and Mrs Clark were Baptists and did a great deal of work for the town and charity. Mrs Clark was a good-looking woman but short and rather stout and had very splay feet. She was a friendly go-ahead person and when she was over fifty she bought herself a car and drove it about in a rather reckless, erratic manner. She worked hard for the Girl Guides and Brownies, often entertaining them at her home. Many garden parties and bazaars were held at 'Rockholme' in aid of the many charities Mrs Clark worked for. I looked forward to the teas at these events as she always provided some of her lovely home-made bread and cakes.

Theo Clark was Mayor three times – 1925, 1935 and 1945. He was a tall well-built man with a fresh complexion, silver grey hair and looked very distinguished in his Mayoral robes. During his first two terms in office his civil functions were very lavish affairs with no expense spared, costing a great deal. But his third term was at the end of the War when there were great shortages and it was austerity for everything. Sadly he died suddenly, during his third term in office. His death was a tremendous shock to his family and friends and a great loss to the town.

One of his twin sons, George, who had worked with him at the Mill, carried on the business. Ted, the other twin, was a Captain in the Army and served with great distinction through the War. When he came home after the War he became one of the owners of the Banbury Guardian.

On the left of the Mill, beside the river, was the Post Office sorting office, which took a great deal of time and trouble to build, as the river-bank had to be reinforced. Now the building belongs to Percy Gilkes the printers.

In the process of writing this book, on 16th March 1992, about 10.30 am a disastrous fire broke out at the Mill which was then a chemical processing plant. It was gutted and nothing now remains.

Between the Mill and the sorting office a footpath led through to the gypsies' encampment, eventually coming out onto a small path, at the end of High Town Road. It was a good short-cut to the hospital from Grimsbury.

Mr Turner, who owned the encampment, had a large high-class fishmongers and fruiterer's shop at 2 Broad Street, selling a wide selection of fish, poultry, game, fresh vegetables and fine fruit.

The Turners lived in a big house, Elm View, Oxford Road. The two eldest sons ran the business but for a long while after he retired, old man Turner and his wife would come down to the shop, where she would sit in the cash desk taking the money and he would interfere with the shop business. There was one daughter, Doris, a tall fair good-looking girl who married Harold Jones of S. H. Jones, the wine merchants. When Doris had triplets, two girls and one boy, it caused a great stir in the town as in those days it was a rare event to have triplets. Harold and Doris Jones received a bounty from the Crown, of a cheque for three guineas, which they never cashed but had framed.

Lower down Station Road was 'Turner's Field', where the circuses were always held. I can remember Bertram Mills, Sangers, Chapmans and many small fairs and menageries there. Before my time, in 1908, Captain Beaumont of 'Queen's Menagerie', came with his troupe of African lions. He challenged anyone to enter the lions' cage. Ernie Bannard, of the boxing club, accepted. When Ernie left the cage he was given a certificate as a memento, which he kept hanging up in his barber's shop. Also, before my time, I was told that Buffalo Bill Cody brought his circus there.

I was always fascinated by the gypsy encampment, and remember it well. It was a dingy place. The caravans were surrounded by a sea of mud and ashes. If you walked by a crowd of dogs always started barking at you until a gypsy would come out and call them off. The gypsies just stared but never said anything as you passed through.

Mr Turner charged the gypsies 6d a day to park their caravans in the encampment. Every Friday he went to collect the rents and if he thought anyone might be moving on without paying, he made extra visits.

Over the years the gypsies' traditional way of life had been changing, and more and more of them were settling in town and starting up businesses, mostly dealing in scrap metal, second-hand furniture and clothes. Some of them have become very successful.

Mrs Houghton was 'Queen of the Gypsies' and she and her large family of six boys and three girls lived permanently in the encampment. Originally she came from Buckingham. Her husband's name was Charles, but I think he had been dead for many years.

The Houghtons had a scrap metal business at the bottom of Station Road and she and her daughters ran a secondhand clothes stall on Banbury Market. If you had any clothes to dispose of, a message to Mrs Houghton brought her and her daughters along at once. She drove a hard bargain but it was cash on the nail and they took the clothes away in a large black pram. They used the black pram for their shopping, filling it up with quantities of the best quality food. They bought big joints of meat, pounds of cheese and butter – the best.

My father Robert Pursaill got to know Mrs Houghton quite well as she shopped regularly in Brown's Cake shop where he worked. She would buy bread, home-cooked ham, large pork pies and the rich Dundee Cake, for which Brown's were renowned. My cousin, Kate Thurstan, who ran a wool and children's clothes shop, would tell me how the gypsies would come in with a crowd of their little children to buy clothes. They bought only the best clothes, paying for them from big bundles of notes kept in a pocket under their aprons. When my father was old and ill Mrs Houghton and her daughters used to come to our front door to enquire how he was. They would never come in although I begged them to as the old man would have loved a chat.

Mrs Houghton ruled the gypsies with a rod of iron and would brook no bad behaviour. A complaint about any of them she would put right at once. Occasionally things would get out of hand when they had had a few drinks. They would start fighting in the pubs. Sometimes it became a near riot with some of the police getting hurt. On one occasion the police commandeered Theo Clark's big lorry, bundled everyone in and took them to the Police Station.

During the 1939 War, several of the Houghtons served in the Army and one of them was a prisoner of war for several years. One gypsy, stationed near Banbury waiting to go overseas wanted to come and see his family, so he took an Army lorry and drove over to Banbury. He drove the lorry over the iron bridge which crossed the river by the encampment. The bridge gave way and the lorry was stuck half on the bridge and half in the water. I don't know what the Army or Mrs Houghton did about the affair but most people in the town thought it was very dashing and sympathised with him. As the bridge was on private property the Council would not repair it, so it remained closed for a long time. If you wanted to cross over you had to walk very carefully over on an iron girder-holding onto the remaining side of the bridge.

Mrs Houghton was a remarkable woman, big, dark and handsome. All her family were dark and striking looking but none had her majestic appearance. She was a clever, astute businesswoman, could read, write and was very good with figures. She looked after all the gypsies' interests. My father said Mrs Houghton told him that she had eventually bought the encampment so that her people would always have a place to live. You would see her striding along Station Road attending to her own and the other gypsies' business. As most of them could not read or write and no accountant would do their accounts, they would bring all their papers to Mrs Houghton. She would put on her glasses, read their papers, do their accounts and fill in the tax forms as well if not better than an accountant.

She died in 1967 aged 84 and is buried in Banbury Cemetery. Her caravan was burnt where it stood in the encampment. The funeral was a tremendous affair and was shown on the National television news. Gypsies came from all around. They all wore new deep black mourning clothes and either walked or rode in one of the sixteen large black Rolls Royces which followed the hearse. Mr Trinder, the undertaker, had had to hire the black Rolls Royces from places as far away as Coventry. The funeral procession stretched from St. Mary's Parish Church to the top of High Street. Wonderful wreaths were piled in the hearse and the top of all the following cars. But best of all was a large throne made of pure white flowers surrounded by lovely wreaths standing on top of the hearse. After her death there was nobody to take her place and gradually the family split up and nothing was ever the same again.

XI 'Barmbry Cakes, Cegarets, Chocolets'

The old Great Western Railway Station was on the left towards the bottom of Station Road where the present station is. Beyond it were the goods yard, cattle pens, great mountains of coal stocks for running the railway and Samuelson's Britannia Works Station Depot, with a tramway for the trucks carrying goods which ran from the Britannia Works to the station depot.

Samuelson's, whom we all called Sammy's, was an important engineering firm with the deepest casting pit in the Midlands. As they employed a great many people, their decline and final closure caused a great deal of unemployment and poverty in the town.

The coal merchants all had their own trucks bringing their coal direct from the collieries to the station yard which was then collected by themselves. Other goods came by freight trains and were then delivered to the customers by the station dray, pulled by a large cart horse. It usually took about three weeks from ordering for the freight goods to arrive at the station. The pilfering was terrible and hardly anything arrived without the cases having been broken open and something lost. The Railway always paid compensation – it must have cost them a great deal. However, things sent by passenger train usually arrived quickly and safely – but it was expensive.

All sorts of small livestock such as racing pigeons, rabbits and chickens were sent by rail in wicker crates. Dogs and small pedigree animals such as lambs, goats or calves travelled muzzled and on a leash and were put in the guard's van. Fish for the fish shops came packed with ice in wooden boxes. The boxes smelt awful and the station would always be left with an aroma of fish. Luggage and other goods went in the luggage van. The goods and luggage on the platforms were moved about on flat wooden trolleys with iron wheels and pulled along by a long wooden handle. When the trolleys were piled high with things, they were so heavy it needed two porters to move them.

The passenger service was wonderful. Trains were punctual, frequent and clean. A fast train from Banbury to Paddington would take just over an hour. The 8.35 am arrived in Paddington about 9.45 am. Several businessmen travelled on it daily; the Quaker bankers, Joseph and Henry Gillett, and the Baron Profumo included. Their uniformed chauffeurs drove them to the station in their big cars. Sometimes Baron Profumo's two daughters travelled up to town with him. They were very tall elegant girls, always beautifully dressed and made up. Occasionally they wore smart riding clothes and expensive looking long black leather riding boots. All the other women passengers were envious and impressed by their beautiful clothes and appearance.

On Tuesdays the 8.35 am had a special cheap day return providing you travelled home in the evening on the 6.10 pm or later. There were also all sorts of other holiday excursions and cheap day trips to interesting places, which my family and I always took advantage of. A Saturday afternoon and evening return to London cost five shillings. As there were one or two trains in the evening you could go up to London for the evening to a dinner and the theatre. Although the slow train leaving Paddington at l2.10 am took over three hours it was useful for coming home after a late night out. It went via Reading, stopping at every little station and wayside halt, to deliver and pick up the mail and drop off the morning newspapers. Very early morning, about 4.00 am other slow trains picked up the churns of milk left at the little stations by farmers for Banbury's morning milk. When the milk arrived, the churns were stood outside the station for the dairies to pick them up. They were known as 'the milk trains'.

The Station itself was built of wood with brick extensions for the refreshment room and bar, waiting rooms and newspaper stands. It was covered by a large roof, open at the top to let out the smoke and steam, so if it snowed or the rain blew in the passengers on the platforms would get wet. In the middle of the station, under the roof, a wooden passenger bridge connected the two platforms. It was open at the sides except for a handrail with trellis work underneath, to prevent the passengers falling off onto the railway lines. If anyone was crossing the bridge when a train came in they were engulfed in steam and smoke and covered in black smuts. For a long while the Station was lit by gas lamps which were lighted by switching them on with a long pole.

Although the Station was dingy and shabby it was full of activity and brightened up by interesting coloured posters pasted on the walls. Posters like the picture of a man in his pyjamas sitting on a large Bovril bottle floating in the sea 'To Prevent that Sinking Feeling', the 'Bisto Kids', smelling the savoury gravy and the 'Kodak Camera Girl', in her attractive blue and white dress standing on a sunlit hill. Some of the adverts were coloured enamel on tin – 'Black Cat Cigarettes' was one of them, others were for Stephens Ink (a big blot) and lots of little plates in blue and white advertising Mazawatee Tea. There were lovely pictures of the seaside and beauty spots advertising excursions. Now all these posters are collector's items.

The general waiting room and ladies' waiting room were big rooms heated by huge coal fires burning in black iron grates. The floors were covered in dark brown lino, sturdy long benches upholstered in black leather cloth standing around the walls, a large table in the middle and one or two big mirrors hanging on the walls. The refreshment room and bar was also furnished in the same fashion but with the addition of marbled topped iron tables and a long dark polished wood counter. On the wall, behind the counter, a huge mirror with shelves fitted across, displayed boxes of chocolates, bottles of whisky, gin and various other drinks. Piles of tired sandwiches under glass domes, stood on the counter, along with a Victorian cash register, a plated urn of hissing boiling water for making tea and a high glass showcase full of sausage rolls, meat pies, slabs of cheap fruit cake and Banbury Cakes.

At one time the refreshment room and bar was let to a Mr G. T. Walker, who employed a manageress to run it, assisted by Mr Eaton. He was a good natured little man with a small round red nose, nick-named by his workmates 'Titty Nose'. He worked very hard doing all the washing-up, cleaning and odd jobs. When the main line trains came in he would rush up and down the platform with a heavy wicker tray hung on a leather strap around his neck. The tray was filled with Banbury Cakes, chocolates, cigarettes and cups of tea. He always shouted 'Barmbry Cakes, cegarets, chocalets', in his broad Banbury accent. He was a well-known character up and down the line and to the regular travellers, who did imitations of his shouting. He sold at least two thousand cakes a week and at holiday excursion time, a great many more.

The two newspaper stands, one on each platform were let to Wyman and Sons Ltd. They were always busy and stocked a wonderful selection of magazines and books as well as the daily newspapers.

The railway carriages were quite different from today's. They were divided into compartments with sliding doors linked by a corridor which ran the length of the train. The seats went across the train. The first class had six seats, three a side. The third class eight seats, four a side. There was no second class, except on very old trains.

The first class was very well-appointed but much more expensive and with no special excursion prices available. There were well-sprung seats, upholstered in good quality plush with white crochet chair backs and fancy spring blinds to pull over the windows. The third class was comfortable but not as luxurious. Both classes had sensible luggage racks above the seats, photos of places that had excursions to them and mirrors on the walls. There was a toilet and wash-basin for each carriage.

All main line trains had well-run restaurant cars supplying excellent meals with waiter service, at very reasonable prices – full English breakfast, morning coffee, three-course lunch, afternoon tea and a four-course dinner. For afternoon tea there were sandwiches, two kinds of bread and butter, jam, fancy cakes and a pot of tea. First class passengers had their afternoon teas served to them in their compartments.

The Great Western Railway was called 'God's Wonderful Railway' and railwaymen or 'railway chaps', as they were known locally, were proud of their jobs which were secure and carried a pension with other benefits, such as convalescent homes after an illness, concessionary rates and free passes for all the family for rail travel and scholarships paid for by the company for clever children to go to the County School.

Although the hours were long, the work hard and sometimes dangerous, there was keen competition for jobs on the railway and when vacancies occurred preference was always given to railwaymen's sons.

The uniforms were heavy, dark blue cloth, well polished black boots, and dark blue caps with slight variations for identifying different jobs. Blue cotton jackets and trousers and shiny black caps were worn for dirty work. Eventually these would turn a grey-blue with all the constant washing.

The drivers, firemen and guards all carried a large black metal box which held everything needed at work. As the hours were so long food would be taken to work. The favourites were bacon, eggs and sausages which they fried on a polished steel shovel held in the boiler fire, with the tea made from boiling water from the boiler, in enamel cans with an enamel cup for a lid to drink from.

A train driver had good pay as it was a very responsible job. They had to have regular medical examinations to see that they were fit. As well as eyesight, the condition of their feet was important. Standing for long hours on a hot footplate tended to give them foot trouble and flat feet. If they didn't pass the medical they were moved to other work.

As railwaymen were often off duty during the day, they had time for gardening and growing their own vegetables. Many kept allotments and were keen gardeners growing vegetables and flowers for exhibition. Chrysanthemums, dahlias and gladioli were the favourites. They entered all the local vegetable and flower shows, winning most of the prizes as their vegetables and flowers were magnificent. All the allotment refuse, old cabbage leaves and weeds, etc were burnt in slow burning bonfires called 'smothers' which smoked away for days and smelt awful. Allotments were social meeting places, almost like a club. There was usually a tool shed made of old pieces of corrugated iron and packing case wood, and for fencing, old Victorian iron and brass bedheads, which had been thrown out when they could afford a nice modern wooden bed. Now these old iron and brass bedheads fetch big prices in auction and antique shops.

In the early 1930s the G.W.R. wanted to enlarge their shunting and marshalling yard, doing away with the footbridge and right-of-way, which went from Spiceball over the railway tracks, to West Street. There was great opposition from Grimsbury people as the bridge was a big short cut into the recreation grounds and the town. It was used by large numbers of people, especially workers who liked to get home for dinner and back again in their dinner hour. Eventually it was agreed that the G.W.R. should do a count on a week day, of the number of people who used the bridge. However, the company waited to do their count until it was a dreadful pouring wet and windy day, when only one or two people crossed over. So Grimsbury lost their short cut and right-of-way. As a sop, the company gave a big donation towards providing Grimsbury with the 'Moors Recreation Ground' but in no way did it compensate for losing the short cut and few people liked or used the Moors.

The G.W.R. went full steam ahead with their plans and built one of the largest marshalling yards in the Midlands. In the middle of the yard they built a hill, called the 'Hump'. Trucks were shunted up to the top and free-wheeled down the other side to the great network of lines fanning out at the bottom where they were then diverted by points to the goods trains. It saved hours of work and enabled the yard to handle huge quantities of freight. The work went on night and day, except Sundays when the yard was closed until midnight.

As it was a long way to the Hump, some men took a short cut through a wooden door on the left of the railway bridge going towards Middleton Road. A flight of steep steps led from the door, down to a signal box and the tracks and then along to the Hump. The door was supposed to be kept shut but sometimes a kind man left it open so that children could watch the trains. It was a splendid view and when my children were young, for a treat we would spend hours at the door watching the trains.

The Station-master's house was on the right side of the railway bridge opposite the wooden door. It was a big square house built well below the road, on a level with the railway lines and the Station. A steep flight of steps led down from the road to the house and a big garden which ran parallel to the railway lines. It has recently been demolished and another empty office block stands on the site.

11. *Interior of GWR Station, Station Approach.*

XII Going, Going – Gone!

Banbury, being a market town, held regular street livestock markets, which had been granted in an ancient public charter. There were street cattle markets held in Bridge Street outside the Town Hall, sheep and horse markets in the Horsefair, while pigs, poultry and rabbits were sold in front of The Angel and The Bear public houses in the Market Place. Iron barricades ran beside the footpaths to try and keep the animals under control and protect the pedestrians.

On market days the roads would be filthy with cow dung which smelt awful and ringworm was rife, which people caught from the cattle. The animals had to be out of the town by 4pm and then the street cleaners got busy hosing down and disinfecting the roads and footpaths. It was dreadful when the herds of cattle were driven into town by drovers, yelling, cursing and beating the poor animals with heavy sticks, which often had nails in the ends. Sometimes a terrified animal ran amok and charged through the streets. Until it was caught and destroyed, people had to shelter inside shops. There is a narrow passage at the end of Newland Place which leads to the back of my husband's old home in Albert Street. Cattle sometimes bolted up it, breaking their horns on the walls and had to be destroyed, as it was too narrow to back them out. It was enough to turn one vegetarian.

You can imagine the smell and congestion in the town with all these animals. There was great feeling in the town that the markets should close and move to a new site. Over in Merton Street where Midland Marts the auctioneers held their own markets was the site that was offered to the town. Before deciding to close the street markets, which were held as an ancient right in a charter, a big enquiry was held in the Town Hall. My mother took a great interest, going to all the sessions, often taking me with her. I was the only child and my mother one of the few women present. The Ministry Inspector sat up in the judge's seat and the floor of the big room was crowded with men, all wanting to speak. The sessions got quite heated as feelings ran high with some for and some against the move. Eventually the Inspector found in favour of Midland Marts and their new sale yard and the opening of a Corn Exchange.

In many ways it was much better for the town when the cattle market was moved to the new sale yard, although it gave Midland Marts Auctioneers a monopoly on all sales of cattle and put all the other cattle auctioneers out of business. With the closure of Banbury Street Cattle Market other businesses were affected. The Red Lion in High Street lost nearly all its trade and the unofficial Corn Exchange in its yard. Eventually the pub closed and sold its site. It was demolished and Woolworths built a huge store there. Other eating places were badly hit as the farmers went to the new sale yard dining room and bars for their dinners and drinks and didn't come into the town much. The small farmers and cattle dealers were badly hit, for the market in the streets was free and they couldn't afford the market dues charged in the new sale yard.

The new market was over the canal bridge and over the railway bridge past the station master's house, on the right, to Merton Street. Down Merton Street was to be found the London Midland and Scottish station and goods

12. *LMS Station, Merton Street.*

13. *Banbury Michaelmas Fair, Market Place.*

yard. It was the end of the L.M.S. line – a quiet little station with only a few local trains but the goods yard was quite busy.

Beside the L.M.S. goods yard a road ran down to the Banbury Gas Light and Coke Co., the gasometers, Bernard Frost Coal Merchant and the Railway Mission Hall. Alma Terrace was on the right, a little further on.

Alma Terrace was a row of five pleasant brick villas overlooking the Station and railway lines. With the advent of the new cattle market the second villa was turned into a little cafe which served good plain dinners to the market men. It was run by a Miss M. Malings. At the bottom of the terrace was the entrance to Midland Marts yard. Here there was the new Corn Exchange, cattle auction ring, dining room and bars serving excellent food and drink as the farmers only liked the best. Branches of the main banks – Lloyds, Barclays, Midland etc, established themselves for the convenience of the farmers.

When Banbury Street Cattle Market was moved to the new improved sale yard in Grimsbury, Midland Marts ultimately became the largest cattle market in Europe. But it was a disaster for Merton Street and the area. What had once been a quiet little street of nice houses with well kept front gardens was now an undesirable place to live. Market days were a nightmare as large herds of cattle would often crash into the front gardens, while being driven along the street, making it dangerous. In no time, the street was a wreck and the value of the houses dropped to almost nothing. A house would be sold for as little as £50, that is if you could find anyone to buy it. Eventually instead of the cattle and the drovers coming down the street the cattle were moved in cattle trucks which made it a little better, but the street was then crammed with heavy traffic on market days.

Generally there were no cattle sales on Tuesday, so in the Corn Exchange on most Tuesday afternoons, Midland Marts held a collective sale of furniture, household goods and odds and ends of all kinds. At the sales they sold everything from a roll of wire netting to a grand piano. The junk was displayed outside the yard and sold first. Then everyone moved into the sale room for the better things. The furniture was stacked around the walls and down the centre of the room, while on a long table, all the glass and small nick-nacks were displayed. The auctioneer sat at a desk on top of the table with all the china, etc, laid out below him. Everyone would pack into the room. The sales were very popular and always crowded. All kinds of people came, country people, towns people, housewives, dealers – all looking for bargains. Most of them never missed a sale.

Mrs Gardener was one who always came. She spent a great deal, buying anything that was going cheap for her secondhand business which was in some old garages in the alley leading out to Castle Street, at the rear of the Flying Horse yard, Parsons Street, before it was demolished to make way for the multi-storey car park. She was a well known figure in the town and at the sales, where she was always called 'Mrs G'. Whatever the weather she wore a maroon beret, heavy brown winter coat and carried a brown shopping bag.

For a time old Mr Jackson was a regular. He was a thick-set middle aged man with strong features and thick bushy eyebrows which he raised to signal his bids to the Auctioneer. He had a fine antique shop at the top of High Street but he had to be banned from the sales as he started out-bidding everyone, buying literally everything, so was ruining the

14. *A Street Market, The Market Place.*

sales as no one else could or would bother to buy anything, leaving him with a monopoly.

E. R. T. Abbotts, who we all called 'Erty', was chief auctioneer, Tom Bentley, was second auctioneer. They both had tremendous voices and went at a terrific speed, so you had to follow closely or you missed things. It was very exciting.

As the Corn Exchange roof was largely glass it was icy cold in winter and boiling hot in summer. The poor auctioneers, sitting high up on the table, suffered more than any of us from the cold in winter and the sun blazing down on them in summer. Besides suffering from the cold or heat I usually got a few large flea bites as well.

Mr Dixon was the clerk, assisted by a young trainee and three or four market men acting as porters. The porters struggled to keep an eye on everything but it was difficult – for as soon as anything was sold, the purchasers started carrying it away. If you bought anything small it was best to pick it up and carry it about with you, or if it was too large, to stand by it in case it disappeared with someone else's goods. I would always leave my youngest daughter Sylvia to guard any purchases while I arranged for transport to take them home. There were no catalogues, no reserves, everything had to be sold. Things usually went very cheaply as most of it was very ordinary but if you looked carefully there were always a few good antique pieces to be had. I bought some lovely things for just a few shillings. With the first bid I ever made I bought four pretty little Victorian bedroom chairs for four shillings. Sometimes, if there was a small sale of cattle on Tuesdays, afterwards the farmers came over to the Corn Exchange sale. The prices were much higher when they came, as none of them could resist a bargain and they ran up the prices. They bought all sorts of strange objects and went home with their cars loaded with things they really didn't want.

Everyone felt sorry when Midland Marts gave up their general auction sales as we all enjoyed them and nothing has taken their place. The cattle market from being the largest in Europe has now declined, along with many of the farmers. There are talks of relocating the market yet again.

XIII   *The Bearded Lady, The Fortune Teller and The Wall of Death*

Banbury Fair was the great event of the year. Nearly everyone went, looking forward to it all year, adults and children alike. In my pictures I have painted a night-time scene with the Fair in full swing, all lit-up and a daytime scene of the Market Place, as it was the rest of the year. Banbury Market is held every Thursday and Saturday. The regular shop keepers in the Market Place can be seen with their goods, displayed on the paving, which were then taken in at the end of the day.

The Fair is held in the week of the first Thursday after the 11th October, in the Market Place and on both sides of Bridge Street, which used to be called the Cow Fair. Nowadays the show people start putting up their roundabouts and sideshows on Tuesday afternoon but in the old days none of the Fair people were allowed into town before 12 noon on Wednesday. They had to line up outside the town boundaries and as 12 noon struck, they raced for the best sites.

Often there were accidents and as the Fair got larger and more sophisticated it became a nightmare for the town officials to keep order and collect the rents, for if trade was poor many of the small sideshows slipped away in the night without paying. Eventually Mr Wilson, the biggest showman and owner of the largest roundabouts offered to rent and be responsible for the whole Fair. Although it meant a big drop in income for the town, the offer was accepted and proved to be a much safer and better arrangement as Mr Wilson knew all the showpeople, so could book the sites and collect the rents in advance and the mad rush into town was stopped.

Before the arrangement with Mr Wilson, about a week before the Fair, groups of showpeople and gypsies started gathering outside the town. The gypsies and showpeople never mixed. You met groups of the gypsies coming through the lanes with their horse-drawn caravans. A man would be driving with the smaller children sitting beside him while the other men, women and older children walked alongside with two or three lurcher dogs. One or two strong little gypsy horses were tied to the back of the caravan and all sorts of pots, pans and kettles were hung underneath it. A few of the caravans were gaily painted and had bright coloured designs but most were dingy and shabby and their owners looked very poor. One of their favourite camping sites was Salt Lane on Bloxham Road, which they left in a terrible mess when they moved on.

Every year the Medical Officer of Health had to go round the Fair inspecting all the caravans to see that no showpeople had any infectious disease. About 1923, some gypsy children were found to have smallpox. Everyone was very frightened and no child was allowed to attend school unless they had been vaccinated. I had to be vaccinated at once as I had not had it done. The vaccination made me ill and I was in bed for ten days with a fever.

In those days the gypsies were still following their old traditional way of life. They moved from place to place on a regular itinerary, going to the traditional Market Fairs and visiting the same farms every year, where they were employed ditch-digging, hedge-cutting, picking fruit, potatoes and brussels sprouts, whatever was in season. The farmer always lost some rabbits, game, chickens and eggs during their visits but as long as it was not too many, he turned a blind eye, for the gypsies were hard workers and he depended on their seasonal labour.

They were a close-knit community; dark, swarthy and unfriendly, liking to pretend they had magic powers and could put a curse on you if you annoyed them. People were rather frightened of them and kept away from their encampments. But really they were simple harmless people who if they knew and trusted you were very loyal friends.

Most gypsy men did some horse dealing, understanding and knowing a great deal about them. They also did horse doctoring and made up horse medicines. The gypsy women wore black boots, long dark skirts with an apron, neckerchiefs, black shawls around their shoulders, topped with a black felt hat or headscarf. They liked beads, gold chains and rings, with both men and women wearing gold ear-rings. All gypsies had their ears pierced when they were little babies.

The women went about in groups from door to door selling clothes pegs, besom brooms and clothes line props, which they made from wood cut from hedgerows and spinneys. They also made and sold bright coloured paper roses and milk jug covers to keep off flies, made of net bordered with crochet and glass beads. When I was very young I remember some of the old gypsy women making pillow lace but even then it was almost a lost art.

Sometimes a gypsy woman came by herself and offered to tell your fortune if you would cross her palm with silver but if you refused she threatened to put a curse on you. Very few of them really could tell fortunes, it was just an excuse for begging. But one gypsy fortune-teller was very famous and had remarkable powers. She was Gypsy Rose Lee, a palmist and clairvoyant who could make amazingly accurate predictions of the future. For many years she came to Banbury Fair. She wore a flowing dress, long scarves tied round her head and neck, strings of beads and gold chains, gold bangles and big gold ear-rings. She always had her tent on the corner behind the Town Hall. The tent was lined with heavy draperies and a velvet curtain hung across the doorway. Inside there were three upright chairs, a round three-legged table with a black velvet cloth and a large crystal ball on it. Outside, beside the doorway, stood another three-legged table with a pair of love-birds in a cage on it. For 2d one of the birds picked out with its beak, from a box, a card, with what was supposed to be your fortune printed on it. This was a real swindle but her reading of palms and crystal gazing were wonderful. So many people wanted to consult her that you had to make an appointment to see her.

Elderly people and women with young children usually went to the Fair on Wednesdays and Fridays, mostly in the afternoon when it was quieter. When I was young I looked forward to the Fair but was frightened of the big roundabouts and crowds of people. So my mother took me in the afternoons. I liked the children's roundabouts, donkey rides, hoopla and some of the little unsophisticated gambling stalls. For years an old man had a children's roundabout of animals, birds and little cars on the corner of Bridge Street and Mill Lane. He stood in the middle of the roundabouts turning a handle which worked an organ for the music and turned the roundabout. An old man had his donkeys in Mill Lane where little children had rides. Another old man had a funny little gambling stall behind the Town Hall. It was a sort of roulette wheel, which he turned by hand. You put your penny on a number and if the wheel stopped at your number you had a little prize.

The farmers and their families came into Banbury on Thursday mornings to go to the Special Beast Market, then came into town for their lunches. In the afternoons the farmers went to the Red Lion or White Lion to have drinks and discuss business, while their wives and daughters would walk around the Fair, buying things from the stalls or having a go on the sideshows. The young farmers, looking very smart in their best breeches, jackets and caps, stood about in groups talking or trying their luck in the shooting galleries. Although they were excellent shots, they seldom won anything as the sights on the rifles were usually distorted.

The old country people came in by pony and trap, horse and cart, or had a ride in the carrier's cart. For many it was their annual holiday to which they looked forward and saved up for. Some of them had their lunches and teas at Brown's Original Cake Shop where the Misses Brown knew them all, as they had been coming to the shop for years. All the people from the country left early as they had a long way to go home through the country lanes. But before setting off many farmers and their families came to Brown's Cake Shop for a slap-up tea. Usually ham and eggs, toasted crumpets, bread, butter and jam, Banbury cakes, lots of iced fancy cakes, washed down with good strong tea. Mr Mawditt's Dining Rooms, 40 The Market Place, was another popular place to eat.

Thursday night was THE time for the townspeople, when parties of friends and families escorted by their menfolk went round the Fair. Our fathers made the Fair much more exciting for us children as they had plenty of money to spend, were good at winning coconuts and prizes at the skittles and quoits and could often ring the bell on the Strength Tester. Special excursion trains ran from Birmingham and Oxford and people poured into the town, including many pickpockets, so you had to be careful to keep your money safe. On Thursday night there were so many people, it was almost impossible to move through the Fair. We had to queue for rides on the roundabouts or to get into the sideshows and the price of everything was doubled.

The noise, lights, raucous music of the roundabouts and crowds of people jostling and pushing was great fun but it often got very rough. I loved it when I was a teenager and went about with a crowd of my friends. We had cardboard 'Toddy Wackers' and hard paper or leather balls stuffed with sawdust on elastic strings, with which we hit one another on the head. Some of the boys put sticks in their Toddy Wackers, which gave you a very hard knock. One year, gangs of lads started throwing soot and chalk at people. The police soon stopped that.

Until I was about ten, an ox was roasted on a spit outside the Crown Hotel, in Bridge Street. It took all night to roast. When it was done people sitting by the spit on benches at wooden tables ate dinners of slices cut from the roast, boiled potatoes and cabbage. I was never allowed to have a dinner but they smelt lovely and cost about 1/6d. Then there were the cockles and winkles stalls which were piled high with heaps of boiled cockles and winkles which were weighed into little paper bags and eaten with a pin, while standing by the stall. Rocky Leach had a stall selling his own made rock, flavoured with raspberry, pineapple, lemon clove or peppermint. There were stalls of pomegranates and pears, which were a speciality to eat at Fair time.

The 'Aeroplane' stalls were very popular, especially with women who often spent all the housekeeping money on them and had to struggle for weeks after to get out of debt. The Aeroplanes were large circular stands. The stall holders stood in the middle of the stand at a counter top which ran round the edge. Attached to the roof was a large revolving arm with a model aeroplane on each end. Names of places were hung round the edge of the roof. The stall holders sold tickets, with place names on them for each turn of the arm and for each turn, there were two prizes. If the arm stopped at the name on your ticket you won a prize. These were usually cheap little things, not the beautiful large china dolls, giant Teddy Bears, sets of saucepans, canteens of cutlery or fine china tea and dinner sets which were on the display for prizes. You could spend a great deal of money on the Aeroplanes.

The stalls selling hot strong tea and lumps of cheap cake have gone, as have many of the sideshows. Now there is no Flea Circus, Two Headed Calf, Dancing Girls, Bearded Lady or Fat Lady. Most of the sideshows were held in miserable little tents badly lighted by paraffin lamps or naphtha flares and the customers all crowded in together. The Flea Circus consisted of some large fleas, tethered by long hairs, on a table. Some of the fleas pulled weeny little carts or jumped when commanded by the showman. The showman picked them up with tweezers and kept them on his arm feeding them on his blood. The Two Headed Calf was a stuffed calf that looked as though the second head had been sewn on. Both shows were swindles and disgusting.

The Dancing Girls show was held in a big tent with the front decorated like a Victorian Music Hall. Outside there were lights, music and a high platform on which four sleazy chorus girls, wearing short frilly dresses and feathered head-dresses danced, between the shows inside the tent. At one end a man in evening dress shouted through a megaphone advertising the show while at the other end a man sold tickets from a box office. There was always a large crowd of men and boys standing in front of the platform looking up at the girls' legs as they did their high-kicking dance. I never went to see the show, or to see the Bearded Lady or the Fat Lady. But I remember meeting one Fat Lady. She was a pretty girl of about 19, who was very self-conscious about being so fat. Her manager used to bring her into Brown's Cake Shop for enormous meals to keep up her weight. My father always found her a quiet corner to sit and eat without people staring at her.

The Boxing Booth was popular with the men and boys. It was held in a large tent with a boxing ring in the middle. A team of professional boxers were employed to give exhibition bouts and fight anyone in the audience who challenged them to a fight. The local men liked to show how tough and strong they were by having a fight but usually were no match for the professionals and got beaten every time. However the members of our local Boxing Club, always challenged the professionals, beating them easily and giving them a rough time.

The Boxing Club was run by Ernie Bannard, who coached and encouraged the members and produced many good boxers. He was a fine boxer himself and had won many cups and medals. When he got older he still ran the club but only refereed the contests. The Club held Boxing Matches in Andy's Garage in Station Road. My father often took me with him to the Boxing Matches which I thoroughly enjoyed. In the late 1920s and early 1930s Johnny Byles and Aubrey Fisher of Bloxham were two of the best boxers. Later on a family of boys called Turpin joined the club. They were all good boxers but one brother, Randolph, was brilliant. He went to America and for a short time became World Champion by beating Sugar Ray Robinson.

The 'Wall of Death' was a thrilling show and was always packed out. It was held in the corner by The Crown Hotel in Bridge Street. It was a large round stockade made of wooden planks held in place by strong steel cables bolted together. It measured about 30 ft high by 30 ft across. Outside, a flight of steep steps led to a gallery running round the outside at the top, which you stood on, looking down into the enclosure. Inside, all around the bottom, there was a sloping wooden ramp about 5 ft wide. A showman on a motor cycle started riding slowly round the ramp, gradually going faster and faster, until he was riding in great sweeps up and down the walls. Then he was joined by a team of riders – some with pillion riders. They wove in and out, missing each other by a few inches. Once a rider had a lion riding pillion. The wooden walls shook and creaked as the riders went round and round. The noise and fumes were terrific.

Although it was dangerous, spectators were always offered a chance to ride pillion or have a go on a bike by themselves. They always failed, until one day some members of the Banbury Motor Cycle Club offered to have a try. At the Wall of Death our local Club members put on a wonderful display which was much more daring and exciting than the showmens' act. They were all asked to join the show but they refused.

Among the Banbury club's activities were grass track meetings held in the summer, on Sunday afternoons on the field, which is now the Rugger Club, Oxford Road. They attracted big audiences and had a large following of fans, including numbers of us young girls who idolized them. Four of the most daring riders were Walter Cheney, one of the owners of Cheney's printing works, John Gardner, who had an ironmonger's shop in Parsons Street, George Hill, whose folk owned Gingers Cycle Shop in Parsons Street and Joe Bush, whose father was a Coal Merchant in Cornhill. Joe Bush was a wonderful rider and later became a well-known T.T. rider in the Isle of Man races.

At Fair time the showpeople's living caravans were parked by the footpaths in the Market Place and Bridge Street behind the sideshows with their horses turned out to grass in nearby fields. Most of the caravans were shabby, poor and uncomfortable but some of the better-off showmen had beautiful caravans.

Mr Wilson's old mother had a luxurious caravan with shining paint and brass work. It was parked in the middle of the Fair, by her son's largest roundabout. She ruled like a queen and his workers had instructions to carry out her slightest wish instantly. Inside, her caravan was kept warm and comfortable by an ornate antique stove. The chairs were upholstered in deep red plush. Nottingham lace curtains hung at the windows. She had a wonderful collection of fine glass, china ornaments and porcelain figures which she had displayed on Victorian mahogany what-nots, shelves and on tables covered by richly embroidered and crocheted cloths. Photographs of her family in gold frames hung round the walls. She would sit by her window watching the Fair, accompanied by her two small pedigree Pekinese dogs and a canary in an elaborate brass cage. When I was small my mother and I went to call on her every year. She made us very welcome, making tea and giving us rich cake. It was great going to see her.

The Bible Society stall selling bibles, tracts and religious pictures always did a good trade. Every year, two old Quakeresses, Rachael and Catherine Braithwaite went round the Fair visiting the showpeople and giving them all a religious tract, which was always kept and proudly shown to the old ladies when they called the following year. On the last night of the Fair, Rachael and Catherine laid on a big supper in the Cadbury Memorial Hall, Bridge Street, for all the showpeople, which was much appreciated as most of the showpeople had not had a proper meal during the Fair. When they left they were all given a small card with a coloured picture of a flower and a text from the Bible printed on it. Rachael and Catherine were old-fashioned and narrow-minded but good kind women and they made many friends among the showpeople who all liked and respected them.

All the pubs, eating places and food shops' were busy during the Fair, especially on Thursdays when they were packed out. The other shops did no trade at all. The shops customers either couldn't get in, because of caravans parked outside or they were busy spending all their money at the Fair. The shopkeepers in Bridge Street and the Market Place had a very hard time. As well as doing no trade, most of them lived above their shops, so had to put up with the noise and smoke until late at night.

The Fair had to be taken down and out of town by early Saturday morning when it went on to Stratford-upon-Avon for the Saturday 'Run-away-Mop'. This meant that the showmen would work all through the night dismantling the Fair. It was hard work putting up and taking down the large roundabouts, but the showmen paid good money to any strong men who were willing to help them. There were always numbers of unemployed men who were glad of the work to earn a little extra money. Sometimes, out of work young men managed to get a regular job with the showmen and went off with the Fair.

The Fair today is very different from the Fairs I remember from the 1920s and up to the last twenty years when it started to decline. The roundabouts are basically the same but modernised, much noisier and more violent. In the past Fairs were noisy but the roundabout music was from pipe organs playing punched paper cards and beating brass cymbals. The power was generated by huge traction engines, which towed the large shows from Fair to Fair around the country. The traction engines were parked in out of the way corners of the Fair. When it was dark it was frightening to go near the black noisy monsters standing, steaming and roaring, in their dark corners. The smoke, red glow and noise from the Fair could be seen and heard a long way off. Although it was often rough, the crowds were always good natured and there were very few accidents.

But today the electronic music with its heavy beat is deafening and instead of the smell of smoke there is an all-pervading, nauseating smell of cooking oil and onions. All the traditional features of the Fair have gone and now it is just an ordinary fun fair.

XIV Unemployment, Urinals and Spiceballs

On the corner of Bridge Street and Mill Lane was a lovely sweet shop which sold every kind of confection you could imagine. Their specialities were fresh made chocolates, filled with clotted cream and luxury chocolates in handmade gift boxes. The shop also had a large wholesale trade supplying most of the small sweet shops in the town and nearby villages. Mrs Malling was the owner and when she retired Mr and Mrs Thornton bought the business and continued to run it on the same lines for many years, until the War and rationing made it impossible.

Opposite the sweet shop on the other corner was the Cadbury Memorial Hall. When the foundation stone was laid in 1876 it was called the 'Temperance Hall and British Workman'. Later the name was changed to the Cadbury Memorial Hall.

James Cadbury, a Quaker, was the prime mover in having the hall built and was the uncle of George Cadbury, the founder of the Bourneville Chocolate Factory. James and his wife came to Banbury from Birmingham and bought a high class grocers and wine merchants shop in the Market Place. However, two years later James became a confirmed teetotaller. In order that his stock of wines and spirits should not be a temptation to his customers, he believed that by the pouring of his valuable stocks of liquor down the drain, he'd be helping them towards abstinence. Eventually he gave up his business so that he could devote all his time to temperance work, promoting the study of the Bible, education and trying to improve the dreadful conditions in the town.

At that time Banbury had no mains drainage or sewage disposal. All the filth and garbage lay in the gutters or ran into open cesspits. The only water supply was from wells which were generally polluted. Every year large numbers of townspeople died in the terrible epidemics of cholera and typhoid which broke out in the summer. James organised a meeting of the townspeople to try and compel the Town Council to provide a proper drainage and clean water supply.

Public opinion at the meeting was so strongly in favour of the improvements that the Council reluctantly had to agree to instal the drainage but said they could not afford a water supply as well. So James and his friends formed the Banbury Water Company, funded by private subscriptions.

Only well-off people had a proper water supply or bathrooms. Most working people's homes had no water supply or toilets, only an outside pump and toilet shared by several houses. James believed everyone should have access to water and be able to wash and have baths. He installed private baths in the Cadbury Memorial Hall. The sign advertising 'Hot and Cold Baths' can still be seen painted on the side of the Hall. He also instigated the opening of the 'Outdoor Swimming Baths' in Mill Fields, which is now called Spiceball.

James was a great believer in education for all and gave all his time and a great deal of financial support to the Methodists when they were building their new school in Grimsbury. He was also secretary to the Crouch Street and Cherwell Schools. In 1860 he organised a science school in Parsons Street where boys could receive a technical education. Among the subjects taken were mechanical drawing, inorganic and organic chemistry, animal physiology and zoology. The rate of success in examinations was very high. For the first three years James paid most of the school's expenses himself.

Another of James's campaigns was for the welfare of animals at markets. He made himself very unpopular by reporting cases of appalling cruelty to animals at Banbury Market, at the Petty Sessions, taking out several private summonses against farmers. He recommended that there should be proper supervision of the Market but it didn't receive much support.

Being a great believer in the power of the Bible, James opened a Bible Shop in Parsons Street and also travelled round the villages on a bicycle selling Bibles. At special town celebrations he gave away large numbers of Bibles to the townspeople and to young couples as wedding presents.

About 1860 James and his nephew Joel, from Birmingham, bought land in Middleton Road which used to be Turnpike Lane and built four fine houses on it, numbers 107, 109, 111 and 113 South Place, Middleton Road. For the rest of his life James lived in number 113. My father and mother lived in 107 for 25 years, 1933-1958 and my husband and I and our five children lived in James's old home, 113 from 1946-1958.

The Quakers and the Methodists were his staunch supporters but his extreme views on temperance and social reforms made him unpopular with the brewers, farmers, many leading citizens and the town officials, so there are only scanty accounts about him in the town records.

It was a great grief to him and his wife that they had no children. The Cadburys were a close-knit and devoted family. He kept in touch by long letters and visited them in Birmingham whenever possible. He often felt isolated and alone in Banbury, especially after his wife died in 1875.

He was an extraordinary man who by his boundless energy and generosity accomplished tremendous improvements for the town and its people. He died in 1888 and the Banbury Guardian had a long account of his work and achievements which ended up:

> 'Notwithstanding how others may have differed from him in certain matters the name of James Cadbury will ever recall to memory a self-sacrificing man, a man with whom the good of his community and welfare of his country lay very close to his heart.'

When we came to Banbury in 1919 the Cadbury Memorial Hall was shabby and dingy but it was a busy useful place, and always fully booked. It was used for all sorts of meetings, concerts, lectures and social activities such as Sunday School and missionary teas and suppers, with the Odd Fellows, Rachabites, Girl Guides, Brownies, Scouts and Wolf Cubs meeting there regularly.

The Ministry of Labour and Employment rented the big hall as the Employment Exchange for the unemployed to 'sign on'. For a long while Mr F. Anker was Officer in Charge. Long queues of unemployed men lined up outside in Mill Lane, waiting for their turn to go in. They went in through the main door, up the stairs to the big hall to 'sign on' or be paid their 'dole'. The women and girls' employment office was in Mill Lane. In those days few women were out of work as there were several busy factories who only employed women and there was always a large demand for domestic help.

For a week every summer, 'Cadbury's Chocolates' hired the upstairs front room for an exhibition of all their products for their trade customers. I always went with my father and was given all sorts of free samples. The private baths still continued to be popular as many households still had no baths.

When the 1939 War started the council took over the building for evacuees and school dinners. Now the Cadbury Memorial Hall is in a dreadful state and almost derelict. I wonder what will happen to it?

The Blue Bird Temperance Hotel was next to the Cadbury Memorial Hall. Joseph Gillett, another Quaker, owned the lease and his wife Beatrice employed a manageress to run the hotel. It was comfortable and clean and popular with commercial travellers who were glad of somewhere homely to stay instead of always having to put up in a pub. The manageress was a widowed Quakeress, Mrs Ethel Dann. She had an invalid son, Gregory, and was manageress for many years. The council took over the hotel at the same time as the Cadbury Memorial Hall. The Blue Bird was demolished a long time ago and for many years the site was a vacant lot, used as a car park.

Number 59 Bridge Street was A. E. Fox, Chemist, and next door number 60, was Mrs Maud Andrews's dining rooms. Her husband, Fred, ran one of the few taxi services in the town. Her sons had the transport business in Station Road, where the boxing club held their contests. Now numbers 59 and 60 have been knocked down to make way for the new road to come through.

Number 61 was the corporation yard, where the dust carts, street cleaners, carts, and all the road mending materials were kept. If you passed by in the late afternoon all the street cleaning carts could be seen standing in rows all clean and tidy with the brooms and shovels laid neatly on top.

Banbury Fire Brigade kept their fire engines in the yard. All the firemen were volunteers. Mr F. Anker was chief fire officer and among the many firemen were Walter Cheney and John Gardner who belonged to the motor cycle club. The firemen wore tailored navy blue jackets with brass buttons and matching trousers which were tucked into calf length black leather boots, with beautiful brass helmets which were polished until they shone like gold.

On the footpath, beside the corporation yard and H. O. White's garage, was a terrible smelling wrought iron and brick urinal. It had an entrance in and a way out. To get away from the smell I used to cross the road to where there was a beautiful Victorian letter box standing by the entrances to Cherwell and to Bywaters Agricultural Machinery Shop, number 3 Bridge Street. For some reason it was left there long after the other old letter-boxes in the town had been replaced. When my children were young, as a treat I brought them to post their letters in it, as they thought it was so beautiful.

In my picture of Bridge Street I have painted the Cadbury Memorial Hall, with a queue of men waiting to sign on the dole; Mrs Ethel Dann standing in the doorway of the Blue Bird Temperance Hotel with her son Gregory being taken for an outing in a Bath chair; No 59, A. E. Fox, Chemist, with the weighing machine on which we always weighed ourselves; no. 60, Mrs Maud Andrews and her dining rooms; a wagon is bringing fresh milled flour from

15. *Cadbury Memorial Hall, Bridge Street.*

Edmunds and Kench's mill at the bottom of Mill Lane; Hunt Edmunds brewery dray is delivering barrels of beer and four county schoolgirls are waiting to cross the road as they are going to the 'swimming baths' in Mill Fields (Spiceball).

Mill Lane begins in Bridge Street between numbers 54 and 55. It used to be a rough place where it was unwise to go alone at night. Halfway down, it turns to the left and comes out beside the bus station in the new Castle Street. On the left side on the corner was the 'Struggler' a pub kept for many years by a widow, Mrs Kathleen Soden. The sign outside was 'Atlas' carrying the world on his shoulders. The pub was used mostly by bargees and the unemployed lads who came to gamble in the pub's back room after they had drawn their dole from the Labour Exchange in the Cadbury Memorial Hall. It was a seedy place, the plain floor boards were strewn with sawdust, with a shabby wooden bar and one or two old benches against the walls.

On the other side of the lane there was stabling for the barge horses. Mr Tuzzio, the organ grinder and ice-cream man also kept his pony there, as did Mr Soden, a relation of Mrs Kathleen Soden, who lived in George Street and was considered to be the best chimney sweep in town.

A small turning opposite the 'Struggler' led to the drawbridge which crossed the canal to Edmunds and Kench's Flour Mill, now Spiceball Arts and Sports Centre. Once it had been an old water mill but had been mechanised a long time ago, so although it was now driven by electricity, it was very old-fashioned.

In the late 20's and early 30's trade was poor and they were struggling to survive the competition from the big milling combines, so were grateful when Clark's and Bradshaw's Mills had too much work and gave them some of their milling to do. All day long their horse-drawn drays went up and down the lane carrying grain and flour. For deliveries to the bakers in town they used an old steam-driven wagon. It had a chimney and a whistle like a railway engine and tooted and puffed its way round the town, causing quite a stir.

Beyond the Mill and over a small iron bridge was the recreation ground, which was nicknamed 'Spiceball Park', as it had been given to the town by a wealthy pork butcher, who made his money from the spiceballs, or faggots, for which he was famous. The spiceballs were made from pigs' lights, herbs and spices, baked under a piece of pig's cawl and were a cheap old-fashioned convenience food.

The park was a wonderful gift, much appreciated by the people who lived in the overcrowded area around it. The area was teeming with life and in its narrow streets there were warehouses, factories and houses all jammed in together. There were no trees and nothing grew. A very few houses had tiny gardens, most having just a dingy back yard and some not even that. The park gave the people somewhere green and pleasant to walk and somewhere for their children to play in other than in the streets. People and children from nearby Grimsbury also liked the park as somewhere to walk and play.

The recreation ground was a big piece of land which stretched from the public swimming baths to the bridge at the end of Bridge Street. There were three entrances, one from Mill Lane, one from the bridge, Bridge Street and the Grimsbury entrance, at the bottom of West Street, which reached the park by the footbridge, which crossed the

16.   *The Struggler's, Mill Lane.*

17. *Banbury Guardian Office, Parsons Street.*

railway lines. The park was bordered on one side by a hedge, the tow path and the canal, while on the other side by the river and a row of small poplar trees with three or four seats under them. The grass was kept well-trimmed and everywhere was neat and tidy with no litter.

In those days people had large families and the older ones had to look after their younger brothers and sisters, so Spiceball was a splendid safe place to bring them to play or have picnics. The picnics were usually a bottle of plain water and hunks of 'bread and pull it' (plain bread) or if there was a penny or two to spare, a little Eiffel Tower lemonade powder in the bottle of water and a smear of cheap jam on the bread. The girls sat on the grass gossiping and nursing the babies with the older babies toddling around them while the boys went off playing football at the far end, near the Mill. It was a happy place and much enjoyed.

XV   The Prophet

The offices of the Banbury Guardian were in Parsons Street and were run by William Potts junior. I remember them from the 1920s, until their move to 46 The Green in 1975 (they subsequently moved again in the 1980s to North Bar).

When I worked at E. W. Brown's Original Cake Shop in the 1930's, the shopkeepers and their employees in Parsons Street were a friendly community, taking a great interest in one another's affairs. We would watch the extra activity when the Banbury Guardian was going to press, with the staff working far into the night. Every morning we would see the brass plates on either side of the main entrance being polished, (the plates were outside the office at 46 The Green), the footpath being swilled down and swept and the office fronts dusted and polished.

The entrance to the office was by two narrow doors, making it rather difficult to get in. Inside, the office was painted dark brown. The floor was plain wooden boards and high desks were arranged around the room, leaving a square in the middle for clients to stand while waiting to be served.

The staff were all male. The men on office duty sat on high stools behind the desks. The door into the printing works was at the back of the room. If there was a problem a man would pop into the works to get the answer. After the main entrance there were two doors, one for the men going to the printing works, the other door was to the accommodation above the office, where the proprietor and his family lived. The next window and door was number 52, Frederick Anker, Insurance Brokers. At the back of the building was a big garden.

Although the Banbury Guardian staff were badly paid, they all stayed for years. One reporter, Mr Woods, had a clever daughter Patricia. Mr Potts paid for her to go to college at Oxford, where she did very well, getting a job with the BBC after she got her degree.

Each week, just as now, the Banbury Guardian was eagerly awaited. The most popular features were the 'Births, Marriages and Deaths' and the 'Sales and Wants' which were all on the front page. As few people had telephones the 'Sales and Wants' were put under Box numbers. The replies had to be sent to the office to await collection by the advertisers. During the Second World War, when there was a great shortage of everything, the 'Sales and Wants' was invaluable.

I remember William Potts as owner of the Banbury Guardian. He was a well-known historian and had a vast knowledge of local history. He was a large, tall man, with a square pale face and a great booming voice. He was engaged to a Miss Orchard for many years but they never married, as they both devoted themselves to caring for their relations. His fiancée, Miss Orchard, was a pretty woman but she had a bad scar on her face where William had accidently struck her with his racquet, while playing tennis, for which he never forgave himself.

Shortly before he died in 1947, William Potts formed the Banbury Guardian into a Limited Company, of himself, Ted Clark, and the works manager, Mr Butler. Finally Woodrow Wyatt obtained the controlling interest in the company before it was bought out by Heart of England Newspapers.

18. *Calthorpe Street – a Coronation Street Party.*

In my picture, outside the Banbury Guardian offices, I have painted Theodore Lamb, who I remember well when we lived on the new council estate on Bloxham Road in the 1920's.

Theodore used to ride into Banbury on a home-made bicycle, trailing a gramophone behind him. He used to play the gramophone and beg for money. He would call regularly at the council houses offering to mend clocks and watches. My mother always found him something to mend and he would sit outside doing the repairs, drinking tea and eating bread and cheese my mother had given him. He seldom spoke, mostly he just grunted. He was not a good clock repairer and charged a huge amount for his work. At other times Theodore rode into Banbury on his bicycle, trailing two or three wooden boxes, mounted on pram wheels, to do his shopping. Into the boxes he piled large loaves of bread, home-cured lard, tea and sugar. Gradually he became more ragged, until he had his feet and legs bound round with rags and wore just two sacks, one with holes cut out for his arms and head and another around his waist, tied on with string. People complained that he was indecent, so the police banned him from the town. After that he went into Brailes, where people didn't mind his attire so much. Older people could remember him when he was a well dressed man, usually wearing a smart straw hat and blazer.

He lived in a field that he owned on the right-hand side of the road to Brailes, just below the turn to Epwell and Compton Wynyates.

Theodore had built himself a queer old shack made out of bits of wood and corrugated iron, with a stove pipe chimney coming out of the roof. Inside he had hollowed out the ground making a sunken room to keep himself warm in winter. Every day, all year round, he bathed in the brook at the bottom of the field. For 2/6d, in the summer on Sundays, he would pose for people to take his photograph. He was a big strong man so he did not have trouble with boys throwing stones or harassing him. But when he got older, several times his shack was damaged by gangs of youths.

In the early 1950s we had a wet, cold summer and autumn and he was not able to gather the berries and roots which he stored for extra food in winter. He became ill suffering from starvation and pneumonia. His family were well-to-do Quaker farmers in Sibford, to whom he was a thorn in the flesh. But he had one friend, a Quaker lady called Nina Dell, who befriended him and gave him a dinner any time he called. She became concerned as he had not been to see her for a while. She got someone to go and see if he was all right. They found him starving and ill. He was rushed to the Horton Hospital. On his admission the nurses were nervous, expecting him to be dirty, verminous and aggressive. But he was spotlessly clean, quiet and very grateful for anything they did for him.

They could not save him and he died a few days later as his strength had quite gone.

He was buried in the Quaker buriel ground at Sibford, where a great number of people attended the quiet Quaker Burial Service.

Theodore Lamb was a great character, quiet and harmless but not able to fit into ordinary ways of living. Some say he was crossed in love, some that he was a woman hater. No one knows for sure.

Norman Blinkhorn took a wonderful photographic portrait of Theodore, with which he won a National photographic award. I think it was entitled 'The Prophet'.

XVI   The Party's Over but the Memory Lingers on

Calthorpe Street or Calthorpe Lane as it used to be called has changed completely. The old houses have been pulled down and the street widened. It had been named after Calthorpe Manor, an ancient Manor and estate, the houses being built on its land. It was a picturesque old street, narrow and steep with the road sweeping up from the High Street and ending in South Bar. It was lined with old stone and brick cottages and terraces of Regency houses with people living and running businesses from their homes. There were three pubs, The Black Swan on the left going up the street, The Globe on the right, with The Plough at the South Bar end.

It may have been picturesque but it was shabby and neglected. Few of the houses had any modern conveniences and many of the stone cottages were barely fit to live in. The Council did very little for the street. When all the roads in the town were resurfaced Calthorpe Street was overlooked and left with its rough old road. The same thing happening when there was new street lighting installed – there were no lights for Calthorpe Street.

The Street had a proud record in the 1914-1918 War. More of their men enlisted and suffered fatalities than any other part of town. When the War ended the residents wanted their street renamed 'Honour Street', in memory of their dead. But nothing came of it.

The 1920's and early 1930's was a time of unemployment and poverty everywhere, but the people of Calthorpe Street were desperately poor. Many were War widows, struggling to bring up their families by themselves, on tiny War Pensions. Most of the women had to take in washing and do rough cleaning to make ends meet. Nearly all the men and boys were unemployed with no hope of getting work. They were desperate, and glad if they could get any odd job. When the Northern Aluminium factory opened, life improved. Although the wages were poor, now there was some hope of getting work.

A great many people lived in Calthorpe Street. It was teeming with life. People had large families, 10 or even 12 was quite usual. It is a wonder how they packed into some of the tiny houses and how the mothers managed with hardly any money, no cookers, hot water or any of the simple everyday things we now take for granted.

Strangers walking along the street were not welcome but if you were known it was a friendly place and everyone spoke as you passed. It was a closed community of neighbours who shared each other's troubles and joys.

By the old stone pub The Black Swan was the Drill Hall which the County School used as their gymn. Later it became a wood-working school. Its front door was in an area off Calthorpe Street known as the Cheney's Yard. The entrance to Cheney's printing works was opposite the Drill Hall front door. There were several small businesses in the yard, Fred Green and his son who did cycle repairs, George Hutchings who repaired lawnmowers and the tin-smith, little Jackie Hutt, a hunchback, who mended holes in kettles or pans for 2d and was always in demand, as no one could afford a new one.

Cheneys are a family firm of printers. They started in 1767 at the Unicorn Inn in the Market Place, later moving to a shop in the High Street, then to Butchers Row and then to the Calthorpe Street works. One night in March 1923 Cheneys was gutted by fire, it was a tremendous blaze which could be seen all over town. People living on Bloxham Road had a wonderful view. They all came out of their houses and the children were got out of bed to see the leaping flames and the great glow in the sky. After the fire Cheneys were soon printing again as they hired empty halls and workshops to carry on business until the works were rebuilt. The Yard and Cheneys are now demolished and Sainsbury's store and car park is built on the space. The other businesses have gone but Cheneys are still well established in the town. Cheneys, one of the oldest family firms of printers in the country, are noted for their quality work. They have a fine collection of 18th century printing and family archives which survived the 1923 fire, as they were stored in a house nearby which was being used as offices.

Further up the street was Mr Hoare's lodging house, next door to Mrs May Knight's general shop – then came Calthorpe Gardens, a pleasant cul-de-sac of small houses with little front gardens. The entrance was between large stone pillars which had been part of the old Calthorpe Estate. Next, Robert Higham's coal business and yard which had been the gate house to the Calthorpe Estate. The Highams lived in Calthorpe Gardens, just behind the business. His son Harold worked with him. His daughter Alice, a good dressmaker, often made clothes for Mother and me. Most of her business though was 'making over', mending and altering old clothes for the neighbours. Now Robert's granddaughter Rosemarie Higham, has had the old gate house beautifully restored and converted to an attractive courtyard and shop, where she sells copper and brass and still runs the coal business.

Some stone garages called the Garage House adjoined the long stone wall, the boundary of the Manor's gardens came next. The maternity nurse, Miss Emma Priest, lived at the end of the street and was always scurrying about carrying her black bag and hurrying off to her patients. There was Allitt the undertaker, and S. G. Shilson a woolstapler, who lived in one of the attractive little Georgian houses facing down to High Street.

On the other side of Calthorpe Street, on the right, coming up from the High Street, was Smith Gascoigne & Sons, who had a fruit warehouse. If the door was open you could see the bananas hanging up to ripen in the dark with gas jets burning to give warmth.

Mrs Girling, a second-hand dealer, lived next door. She was a scruffy old woman and everyone called her 'Shooky Girling'. She had four little black dachshunds which followed her everywhere and she loved them dearly. A simpleton youth, supposed to be her nephew, lived with her. His name was Ray. He was tall, strong and good natured and always wore a funny old brown felt hat, turned up all the way round. He always had a crowd of little children following him about. He did all the jobs for his aunt and every morning he piled an assortment of old cookers, mangles and grotty old furniture onto the footpath and every evening he got it all in again. He carted all the things 'Shooky' bought or sold on a large wooden handcart and pushed round a wooden box on four old pram wheels when he did the shopping. When 'Shooky' died he had to go to the Workhouse but settled down happily and was soon doing jobs for the Workhouse Mistress who found him very useful.

A little higher up, there was Mrs Sophie Gascoigne, who had a fruit and vegetable shop. Next door was Asa

19. *Calthorpe Street.*

Cleaver's bakehouse. It was a thriving business and he and his sons Harry and Fred baked beautiful bread. Asa Cleaver's cousin was Theodore Lamb. Theodore would always buy his bread at his cousin's shop but if Asa saw him he would shout at him, 'Get out you dirty old devil and wait outside'.

Asa's daughter, Doss Cooper lived next door to him. She was a War widow with two small daughters, Dolly and Naomi. Doss was supposed to help in the bakehouse but wasn't much good at baking, so delivered the bread, pushing an immensely heavy covered handcart. Cleaver's had a large bread round and she must have been very strong to push the great cart, loaded with fresh bread, even pushing it up Bloxham Road hill. Doss would shout greetings to everyone she passed. If she and my father-in-law met they always enjoyed shouting insults at each other and exchanging smutty jokes. She was a small woman with a mop of curly red hair, always cheerful and a great character.

Then there was The Globe Inn. A pub no longer, the Globe Inn is still standing. The back has been redeveloped and it is now an office. It is a listed building so the front has been preserved and beautifully restored and it looks very fine.

Then there was Mr J. W. Humphris the barber. He charged 6d a time and did the cutting in his front room, which was always crowded with men waiting for a haircut. Then there was George Hutchings, the Town Crier. He lived in one of the last houses. For Town Crying he wore a black three-cornered hat and a long black coat and he rang a large handbell as he cried out the news – sometimes while riding his bicycle! The Plough Inn was right at the end of the street but I have forgotten what it was like.

Right at the top of Calthorpe Street, on the right was the yard of Withey's dairy, where they kept the milk churns and delivery van. Stanley Withey's Dairy was in South Bar. Stanley was married to Dolly, who was Doss Cooper's widowed daughter. Dolly was a hard working woman who ran the shop, did the accounts and helped Stanley wash the empty bottles and fill them with the fresh milk from the churns at 3 am before Stanley went out on his rounds. It was a very happy marriage.

In the bay window of their shop was a beautiful large white china swan with fresh eggs displayed between its open wings. There was also a model of a golden cow and several fine potted ferns. Outside was a machine, which for a sixpenny piece dispensed half-pint cartons of milk, when the shop was closed. Our family were always being despatched up the hill in the evenings to get milk as we'd run out. George, my youngest son, would be sent if we had no sixpenny pieces, as he would have to disturb the Withey family to sell him some milk – Mrs Withey had a soft spot for George so didn't mind opening up.

However hard the times, National events such as Coronations, Jubilees and Royal Weddings were always celebrated. Doss Cooper usually made the decorations and everyone chipped in with what they could manage towards the festivities.

By 1953 people in the street were no longer poor, as now there was plenty of work. So for Queen Elizabeth's Coronation it was decided that they would hold the biggest and best celebration ever. They hired a loudspeaker system, put up expensive and elaborate street decorations, and arranged a large supper and dance for the adults, with a tea-party for the children. Every child was given a present and a grand paper hat. It was a splendid affair. Theirs was the best decorated street and the best celebration in the whole town. In fact it inspired them once again to ask to have their street renamed, this time Coronation Street – but as usual nothing came of it.

Calthorpe Street is nothing now – just a road with car parking spaces and many empty modern offices. It was an attractive street and would have been most desirable today, but nobody tried to save it, and it has all been demolished except for the gate house and The Globe.

The people who lived there were respectable and hard-working who succeeded in spite of having to overcome terrible poverty, over crowding and bad housing. Any one with roots in Calthorpe Street should feel proud. They were wonderful people.

20. *The White Lion Hotel, High Street.*

XVII And They're Off!

My husband's family, the Lesters, originally came from Chatteris in Cambridgeshire. They had a chequered past and for a time lived in the East End of London. Of this generation, I remember my husband's grandfather, William – 'Will' – born in 1851. He married twice. By his first wife, Elizabeth Bates of Guernsey, he had seven children. William, Horace, Rose, George Washington, Lily, Spencer Henry, known to his family as Tib, and Charles Edward. And by his second wife, he had a further eight children, the last being born a year before his death in 1934 at the age of 84. I'm sure not many people in their 50's can say their father was born over 140 years ago.

Will Lester was a tremendous character and personality. A physically large and strong man, who somewhere along the line had received a good education and could read and write, he had an eye for quality, which his sons inherited. He was a tyrannical parent who beat his sons, throwing them out of the house when they reached the age of seventeen, to make their own way in the world, but treasuring his daughters as precious jewels.

He worked in the Victoria Docks, a job at that time which was much in demand. When a vacancy fell, you literally had to set to and fight – the strongest going to the top of the queue. His pastime and passion was horse racing.

The family seemed to have always had a keen interest in horses, racing and betting. Will went in for 'Ready-Money' betting on street corners. It was illegal and if you were caught you went to prison. Horace, who worked at the Tate and Lyle sugar factory, went into 'business' with his father taking street corner bets. One time though, Horace was caught by the police. The other two elder boys went to sea. William travelled all over the world and George Washington led a colourful life, gun-running and smuggling in the South Seas, gold prospecting in Australia, where he was known as 'Whitie', and amazingly walking across the Kalgoorlie desert. I believe, just because it was there.

Around this time Will mysteriously got together a lot of money and moved the family to Leighton Buzzard, where he had bought racing stables, becoming a legal bookmaker while still continuing the practice of 'Ready Money' bets. The business thrived. Young Charlie exercised the horses on the Downs while Will ran the business, travelling around the country picking up customers and cutting a dash in the local pubs. One of Will's customers was a Thomas Charles Viggers, landlord of the Criterion pub in High Street, Banbury. They became firm friends and Thomas persuaded Will to move to Banbury, which he did, settling in Britannia Road about 1910.

Charlie and Tib, being around the age of 17, followed their father and Horace into bookmaking, all four having separate businesses, both legal and illegal. Tib was not succesful so Charlie took him into partnership. By the age of 19, Charlie had married Thomas Viggers' only daughter, Henrietta, and had bought a house, 26 Albert Street, from where he ran his business. Their subsequent son Charles Junior, I married.

Charles Edward was a brilliant sportsman and could have been a professional footballer, cyclist, bowls or billiard player. But sad to say like many of his family he was lazy and squandered his talents.

21. *The White Lion Yard.*

22. *Corpus Christi procession.*

Horace Spencer Lester and his second wife Annie Stroud of Mild May Farm, Grimsbury, had six children. Horace, Ernest, Joan, Spencer, Geoffrey and John. Horace and Annie were doting parents with no expense spared in their children's upbringing. They had elocution lessons, piano lessons and dancing lessons and Ernie in particular was a very talented dancer. They took part in all the local charity shows and concerts and were well known for their dancing displays and beautiful costumes. They were always beautifully dressed for everyday, usually in matching outfits. One time it was sailor suits, another time their clothes were luxury velvet suits with lace collars and cuffs for the boys, with a velvet dress with lace collars and cuffs for Joan. Annie used to buy the very best toys from Hamleys in London. They had a rocking horse, Meccano sets, beautiful books, everything you can think of. They had a playroom on the ground floor which led out onto the garden but even though Annie had nursemaids and a nurse, she always liked the children with her and under her care. Annie was very kind to our children, and often had them to tea, and would give them lovely Christmas and birthday presents – she was a most generous person.

Employed in the house were a uniformed nanny and nursemaids, resident cook and maid, several daily women who came in to do the cleaning and laundry and a full-time gardener. The garden was large but mostly a huge vegetable plot with two large greenhouses. Vegetables were grown for the house, while three allotments elsewhere were devoted to potatoes. In the greenhouse, tomatoes and cut flowers were cultivated, especially carnations. Every day Horace would have a fresh carnation for his buttonhole.

Food was never stinted in their household. There were always large joints of meat on the table, a choice of mutton, beef and pork, with Horace sitting at the head of the family table, carving the joints. At tea-time the table was loaded with cakes, six or seven different varieties, jams, many kinds of bread and potted meat, and open house to all friends and visitors. The house-keeping expenses must have been enormous but although Horace complained about them bitterly, I think that secretly he was very proud of the good show Annie always put on. He himself was not slow in being forthcoming in hospitality. Anyone who called would be offered good quality spirits and wines. One of his weekly visitors was old Doctor Dwyer who called in every Sunday after church to have a drink with Horace. And at any celebration Horace, like his other two brothers, Tib and Charlie, would entertain lavishly.

The family lived at 'Sunloch', 121 Middleton Road. Horace called his house Sunloch, as he founded his fortune when he put everything, literally everything he had on a horse called Sunloch, which fortunately won and made him a great deal of money.

A wealthy bookmaker, an accomplished billiard and bowls player and a keen Mason, Horace was well known in racing circles all over the country and as owner of several successful racehorses. Horace was a very shrewd businessman and everything he touched turned to gold. He ran his huge business from a small back room in Sunloch and the ground floor of the house next door – 119 Middleton Road. He employed eight clerks, who took bets over the phone, worked out the winnings, writing out and adding up the weekly accounts. In those days there were no calculators to help them, so they had to work out everything for themselves. Everything had to be on a weekly account with 'settling' day on a Monday.

Racing to Horace was more of a hobby than a business. He was a very successful backer and made a great deal of money. When he attended race meetings he took parties of his men friends with him. They always went in one of his great big cars which he would drive at high speed. If Horace had had a good day at the races, he used to come back and fetch out champagne for everybody. They had no end of visitors staying overnight and visitors calling during the day. It was a house full of life and activity.

Horace loved great big black cars and usually had a Rolls Royce limousine and a large Daimler, which were kept in a garage at the bottom of the garden. Every day, dressed in a dark tailor-made suit, black silk tie, black overcoat, bowler hat, a diamond tie-pin sporting a large diamond ring and smoking an expensive cigar he would be seen driving up town. His first port of call was the Conservative Club, followed by the White Lion Hotel, where he usually met Annie. A drink and then a drive home to lunch. He was a dashing figure, tall, well-made, with grey curly hair and moustache – a real spiv!

Prosperous bookmakers' wives were well dressed, and Annie was no exception. Her everyday clothes were quality tailored suits; for evening occasions she wore gorgeous expensive velvet dresses, usually in black or a rich jewel colour to show off her beautiful jewellery. The jewellery would be taken from the safe and, at the end of an evening out, returned under lock and key.

Charles and I had no expensive clothes and jewels but we often were taken to local Masonic Ladies' Nights and to several of the top London Lodges of which the Lester brothers were members. Horace, Tib and Charlie, would take big parties of us to London with all expenses paid.

Our clothes for the evening would be packed in suitcases. Wherever the event was, the Dorchester or Savoy – the best hotels – suites would be engaged for the evening. One suite for the ladies to rest and change clothes, the other suite for the gentlemen.

We also went to the Victoria Club's Annual Banquet and Ball given each year in honour of the owner of the Derby winner. The Victoria Club was a famous racing club and stood on the corner of Wellington Street, opposite the Mecca and just off the Strand. But women were barred from the Club, so, for the Derby winner, there would be a Ladies Night, usually held at the Savoy. It was great fun to see all the bookmakers such as William Hill and their guests in their beautiful clothes, with the wives dripping with magnificent diamonds and precious jewels. There would be a banquet and cabaret, followed by the ball. Each year the guest of honour was the owner of the Derby winner. One year it was Tom Walls, the stage and film star, who owned the Derby winner. Another year it was Edgar Wallace, the celebrated crime writer.

I remember how the day began. We'd have breakfast and lunch at home as usual, then when on the train to London, we'd probably have full afternoon tea. After changing into our finery in our suite we would go to the banquet. On the table, throughout the meal, would be many different kinds of rolls, Melba toast and butter. Each of the courses would have a different kind of wine suitable for fish, flesh, fowl, sweet or savoury. Each would be served with the appropriate kinds of vegetables or fruits. It must be remembered that these were the days before freezing and food preservation. What today may seem mundane, was a luxury item. Many of the foods would have been grown in heated greenhouses or have been flown in from the continent. There would be out of season peas, french beans, runner beans, cucumbers, endive, salads, new potatoes, nectarines, strawberries, peaches and many other kinds of fruit. All would be the very best you could imagine, small, young, choice.

The banquet would begin. . . . To start, oysters with brown bread and butter, which was a hot favourite with nearly everyone except me; one year an extra course of caviar and endive which I remember so vividly, as I had a worm crawling on the plate and the waiters nearly fainted with horror. Then the next course followed: a consommé soup with sherry; next hors d'oeuvre, followed by a fish course with a rich sauce; a breather while we had a sorbet appetiser; next an entrée – lamb cutlets or similar lightly cooked meat; then asparagus with a rich sauce followed by the Roast; next sweets – a choice of wine-jellies, frozen puddings, trifles, Chantilly creams. Then cheese and biscuits and coffee served with petits-fours, of fruits dipped in caramelised sugar, tiny eclairs, meringues, almond biscuits, little sponge cakes soaked in liqueurs and dipped in fondant icing, small, dainty and served from wonderful spun sugar baskets. And finally came brandy and liqueurs. At the end of 10 or more courses the ladies would receive a presentation, an identical but very expensive gift from the men of the Lodge or Club. The gentlemen would then retire to the bar while the ladies adjourned to the ladies room. A rest!

Meanwhile the Banqueting floor would be cleared in preparation for the dance. It wouldn't be just any old band playing. Depending on the grandness of the Lodge it would be the top band of the day, like Geraldo. After whirling around for a while – halfway through the evening – the dance floor would be cleared again for the cabaret. After which it was time for the buffet to appear.

It would be a splendidly laid table with amazing spun sugar baskets and other decorative sugar creations. The table would be laden with smoked salmon and chicken sandwiches; lobster and oyster patés; prawns in aspic; eggs in aspic; chicken and turkey galantines; smoked ham; salads; asparagus rolls; small sausages, great varieties of fruits; wine jellies; petits-fours; exotic fruit cups laced with liqueur and lemonades . . . the dance would begin again . . . and so to the end of the evening.

At the end everyone would retire to their suites packing away their fine clothes in their suitcases for the return home. There would always be a mad rush to get a taxi to catch the 1.30 am train from Paddington. It got into Banbury just about the same time as the mail train – 3 am.

While waiting for a taxi in the foyer of the hotel, cups of hot soup would be offered round. Any party who had come a long way for the evening need only ask, and a waiter would bring an enormous packet of smoked salmon sandwiches or the like to fortify the travellers on their way home. On arriving home the more mature members of the party would take warm milk before retiring! How we ever ate all that food I'll never know. One learned that it was inadvisable to eat all of the courses, especially in the beginning, and to avoid the bread and butter. The courses were only small portions but the roast chicken or quail would be a whole bird. Admittedly there were those who ate and drank absolutely everything, solidly, through an evening but I can't remember anyone being particularly fat or overweight as they are today. I only know that in no way could I ever again find the strength to dance and eat my way through such a day. This is where the Lesters came from. They were a colourful family who had raised themselves from a terrible, rough, poor background to become successful astute businessmen.

The Lester brothers were regular customers at the White Lion and if Charles and I had enough money we would treat ourselves to an evening dinner there. The White Lion was the best hotel in town. It was owned by Tom Page. He was a tall distinguished looking man who spent most of his time out hunting or riding. He had a great big dapple grey horse and always wore grey riding clothes, a bright yellow waistcoat, a carnation in his buttonhole and a very smart grey bowler hat. His wife was a great deal younger than him. They had three daughters. Mary, a pretty little thing who was very religious, and the other two, Sally and Betty, tall distinguished looking girls who looked like their father. One of them was very good at sports, being a junior golf champion.

Although Mrs Page was only 19 when she married she was a most capable young woman, and her husband, who was years older than her was really rather an ornament, but an excellent host, left to her the running of the hotel. She did all the accounts and the bookings, was an excellent cook and did all the cooking, making the White Lion famous for its comfortable accommodation and its fine food.

Inside, the hotel was beautiful. It was furnished with magnificent antiques. The bar and bar parlour in particular were wonderful. Around the walls there were beautiful old Windsor chairs. The Windsor chairs were made especially for individual men customers. They had to sit on a piece of sand so that the old chairmakers could make a template so the chair was entirely comfortable for them. There was a shelf which ran around the top of the walls, which housed beautiful great pewter plates and rows of pewter tankards engraved with customers' names. Of course, all the pewter was not used in modern times, just used for decoration, but it was all immensely valuable and made a wonderful décor. Upstairs there were not many bedrooms but they were very comfortably furnished. In the main bedrooms they had large five foot old brass bedsteads with brass rails running round the top for hanging the bed curtains.

The White Lion was a very exclusive, quiet hotel. There was no raucous music and everybody behaved in a very stately manner. The regular customers used to sit in the bar or in the lounge where they met every evening. It was all very dull and rather gloomy. It was like a private club and they used to sit round in the bar or the lounge drinking their drinks and talking in quiet subdued voices. There was no rowdy behaviour and nobody ever got drunk.

There was extensive stabling in the yard which led to the 'White Lion Tap' which came out into Church Passage. Tom Page used to stable his horse in the stables behind the hotel. The stables, the odd jobs, the hotel-portering, were all done by Dickie Manning. He was a dwarf and he had an immensely deep voice and was very strong. He was devoted to Mrs Page and used to help her in the kitchen. She had huge gas ovens for cooking her meals and when they needed cleaning Dickie would actually climb into the oven. In the yard along the side of the hotel was a famous wisteria, reputed to be the longest in the world. It bloomed twice a year and was a wonderful sight to see.

Eventually Tom Page and his wife and daughters sold the White Lion and retired. They went to live in a large house on Oxford Road and their daughter Sally married a local doctor. When the White Lion was sold they had the most tremendous auction sale and the antiques and pewter fetched very high prices. Not only did the customers want mementoes of their old hotel but the things were so valuable. The antique dealers from London were so excited about the old oak Windsor chairs and joynt stools.

The White Lion was bought by the Jones brothers and by Mr Kimberley, employing a wonderful manager, Mr Jim Thewlis. He came from the famous Trocadero restaurant in London. It was almost in line with the Ritz. I don't know if he had shares but he was a wonderful manager and he and his wife lived on the premises.

In the AA and the RAC books there was special mention of the cuisine at the White Lion. They didn't have enough bedrooms and bathroom facilities to warrant the full star treatment but they had a special mention for their wonderful food. On Saturday nights you had to book well in advance or you couldn't get a table. They had an Irish head waitress. She was most efficient and she used to make wonderful Gaelic coffee, which she prepared made at the table. I have never tasted anything so beautiful. Mr Thewlis was always about, always on duty. They also did excellent receptions and parties. The Northern Aluminium Company always had rooms reserved there permanently, so that they could put up their visiting experts and important visitors. It was very popular and made a great impression on their guests as it was friendly and informal and there was always somewhere comfortable to sit. Mr Thewlis would always provide pots of tea and trays of sandwiches at any time. It wasn't like a hotel at all.

Sadly the White Lion changed hands again. Mr Thewlis left. The yard and stables were sold and what is now the White Lion Walk was built. The wisteria can still be seen though, but it is not the magnificent tree it once was. A specialist had to be called in to try and save it, as it begun to die when all the new building was started. For a time the White Lion continued as a hotel but with no success. The Council used it for DSS people with nowhere to live but now it stands empty and closed.

The White Lion was the last coaching inn to go in the town and I find it very sad that Banbury never seems to retain any of the town's landmarks and meeting places.

XVIII   Trials and Tribulations

James Cadbury built 113 Middleton Road for himself and lived there until he died in 1888. It was by far the most comfortable of the terrace of four houses; well insulated, with wash-basins in the bedrooms, three inside toilets, two bathrooms and with only the kitchen arrangements being poor. James took a great pride in the garden and designed the layout himself. There was an attractive paved area outlined with small box hedges, three large rockeries, two nice lawns, a long herbaceous border and space for some vegetables. He planted four Orange Blenheim and Bramley Seedling apple trees, besides many other kinds of fruit trees, bushes, ornamental shrubs, trees, espalier trees of dessert plums, peaches and pears. There was a big heated greenhouse and a wooden summer house, which was large enough for six or seven people to sit in and enjoy the garden.

The garden was used for meetings and social gatherings of all sorts, including Methodist Chapel meetings and teas for the children of the Sunday and day schools. It gave him great pleasure to entertain them for although a Quaker he felt in sympathy with them. When they built their new school in West Street, James helped them raise a great deal of the money and also gave a large donation. The non-conformists, who were virtually barred for 150 years from University education, knew the value of schooling. Schools such as the one in West Street were common, flourishing and successful enterprises around the country. I have painted another non-conformist church, the one in Marlborough Road, as its schoolroom was demolished and the land became part of Sainsbury's car park.

After James died, 113 Middleton Road had several owners before it was bought by William Welford, a retired coal merchant, a short stout man with white hair and a small pointed beard. He and his wife had two grown-up children, a son and daughter. Their daughter, tall and slender like her mother, lived with them and nursed her invalid mother. The son had married, but it was a happy united family and he would call in every day to help with the care of their parents.

The Welfords loved the garden. Mrs Welford would spend a lot of her time resting in the summer house while her daughter pottered about, picking fruit that was in season and Mr Welford, dressed in an old Panama hat, white apron and a pair of large gardening gloves, worked hard at the maintenance.

Everything was kept in beautiful order. There were no weeds, all the fruit trees and bushes were correctly pruned and the greenhouse was always full of plants and flowers. A full-time gardener/handyman was employed to help Mr Welford, and most days the two men could be seen working together in the garden or greenhouse.

Like everyone else during the War, the Welfords had evacuees billeted on them. Theirs were nice teachers who stayed with them until their school pupils returned to London. Miss Welford now alone after the death of her parents, also let rooms to a young couple with a baby. In 1946, just after the War, Miss Welford decided to move to a smaller house and put 113 Middleton Road up for sale, for £2,750.

Although it was more than we could afford, Charles and I wanted the house very badly. We just managed to scrape up enough to buy it, pay for the fixtures and fittings and the costs, leaving ourselves with £30 in the bank. As there was an acute housing shortage and all empty houes were being requisitioned, Miss Welford had to move into a new house at once and Charles had to camp out in our new house while we waited for the contracts to be signed and we could move in.

We loved our new home. It was much too big for us and our three little children, Helen, Anne and Charles nicknamed Tarka. We could barely afford the upkeep, had little furniture, no stair carpet for the long flight of stairs, no floor coverings except for six small rugs, only six pairs of little cotton curtains, which were much too small for the big windows – but it was of no consequence. Miss Welford left hanging at the windows some old curtains and some lino on the floor which was so old it might have belonged to James Cadbury, and we were grateful. At that time our shabbiness and lack of furniture didn't matter too much as after six years of war and shortages most people's homes were shabby and needed decorating. Even if we had had the money we couldn't have bought anything, as everything was rationed or on points. Only people whose homes had been bombed and newly married couples were given a few points to buy what little was in the shops.

I ought to explain that 'points' were a system of rationing. Ordinary ration coupons entitled you to so much per week of a particular item, sugar, meat, bacon, lard, butter and so on. 'Points' were different. You had so many points per month and you could use these at your discretion. for example, a tin of sardines might be 15 points, or a tin of Spam 30 points. You had to be very careful and cunning how you spent them. Later in the war and post-war points were issued for household items. Clothing was also rationed on a system similar to points, as were sweets. After the War bread was rationed for a time. The bread coupons were called BUs.

Providentially we took out a large insurance on our new home. We had only been there for eight days when there was a terrible gale, which loosened both the huge chimney stacks, blowing off the chimney pots and a great many of the slates, blowing a ten foot wall at the end of the garden into South Street and also blowing down the dividing wall which belonged to us. The insurance company paid for everything except the dividing wall, which they claimed was in poor condition anyhow. It was a very narrow escape as there was no way we could have afforded to do the repairs.

That winter was one of the coldest on record. For weeks, thick snow lay on the ground and deep drifts blocked all but the main roads. A searing east wind blew continually down Middleton Road and everything froze, including water supplies to the houses. Ours was the only house in the street whose water supply was not frozen. We had a procession of neighbours carrying buckets to the front door, begging for water until the water cart started coming round twice a day with water. The cart stopped every thirty or forty yards, always coming at the same time, so people could be ready with their buckets and tubs to collect their water.

There were also no deliveries of coal as the yard was empty – nothing could be brought from the collieries as the sidings and points were frozen. Our big house was unbearably cold and we had no means of heating it except with coal fires. When Miss Welford left, she sold us her stock of coal, so for a short time we managed to keep a small fire in the kitchen and in the afternoons and evenings a fire in the sitting room.

We tried living in the kitchen, but it was too draughty and uncomfortable, so we encamped upstairs and made a bed-sitting room in the big front bedroom, where there was an old enclosed Siesta stove, which Miss Welford had left behind. It was black ornate cast iron, had two doors with mica windows and was very ugly. We had nearly thrown it away when we had moved in. But it now proved invaluable. It burned night and day giving off a steady heat and using hardly any coal. My mother lent us a few blankets and dust sheets to screen the landing from the draughty stairs and at night we left the bedroom doors open, so keeping both the front and the back rooms warm.

To keep some heat in the kitchen, Charles dug out all the old slack from the back of our huge cellar, damped it, wrapped it up tight in newspaper with tea leaves and kitchen scraps and made parcels of fuel. With them we kept a tiny fire burning all night in the kitchen grate to stop the back boiler from freezing. It stayed bitterly cold and still there were no coal deliveries. We had burnt the last of the slack and the cellar was swept clean except for one large lump of coal, just enough to last a day, when suddenly some coal was delivered. We were overjoyed as we had been worried how we should manage when the last of our coal had gone.

We also had to contend with frequent electricity power cuts and breakdowns. The cable had needed renewing before the war, so by now it was in a terrible state. The electricity went off without any warning three or four times every evening and as we had no candles we had to sit in the dark until the lights came on again. We heated the scullery with our only electric fire which we had bought during the war for 16s 3d. It barely glowed red and gave off hardly any heat but it kept the place from freezing. There were no power points in the house so, although it was dangerous, we ran the fire off the electric light with a long flex. Added to this the gas supply was awful. The plant was about 100 years old and was quite inadequate to supply all the houses that were now in Grimsbury. The pressure used to drop away to almost nothing and it took ages to boil a kettle or cook a meal. But somehow everyone managed to struggle through.

It was wonderful when the thaw came. But that brought terrible trouble with burst pipes causing a great deal of damage. We were lucky as none of our pipes had frozen. But we didn't escape the effects of the thaw, for as the snow melted it cascaded off our roof, crashing through the glass roof of the lean-to scullery and the porch over the dining room French doors. It was impossible to find anyone to mend it, so Charles patched it up with old pieces of wood, cardboard and lino which we had begged from my mother.

It was a beautiful spring. Everything turned green and the trees were all covered with blossoms. We thought our troubles were at an end. Wrong! One after another the children came down with chicken-pox, then German measles and finally little Charles had measles. I was expecting our fourth baby and was quite unwell and supposed to rest. Of course it was impossible and we were always calling in the Doctor.

On September 9th, 1947, I had a great big baby boy. He was a good-natured happy baby and was no trouble at all. We called him George and everyone, including our dog Rom, loved him. There was no National Health Service then. We had to pay for everything – the Doctor's visits, the care, the treatment and my confinement. The bill for the six months came to £34, about £1,200 today – but Doctor Wharton was very good to us. He knocked a great chunk off the bill and told us to pay when we could manage it.

My fourth child was a very different experience from my first. In 1936 when I was expecting my first child Helen, I was living in Leamington Spa. As soon as I thought I was pregnant, I registered at the Wharncliffe Hospital Maternity Wing. It was essential to book at once, as the hospital had a wonderful reputation and beds were scarce – although a bed was always available for emergencies. They held an ante-natal clinic one afternoon a week, in a room which would be packed with women, in all stages of pregnancy, sitting on benches. There were two curtained off corners where you undressed and put on a white hospital gown, tied at the back of the neck and open all down the back. No one had any false modesty. We would all laugh and joke about our figures and how awful we looked. There was a curtained cubicle where we were examined and our record cards filled in. At first we were examined every month, then every two weeks and finally every week. If it was thought necessary, you were taken into hospital for a rest in bed, or if there might be complications, you had to go in well before the confinement date so that you could be under observation.

A weekly thrift club was held at the clinic, to which we were encouraged to go and to pay in what we could afford towards the cost of our coming confinements and surgical supplies. The confinement cost about £5 for everything – including a nine or ten day stay in hospital. At the club we had cups of tea and biscuits, chatted and compared notes with the other women and got acquainted with the Doctors and Nurses.

Just before my baby was due, we had to move back to Banbury, which still had no maternity facilities – only the District Nurses. Some of them were kind and helpful, but many were rough and bullying to their patients, shouting at women in labour or even hitting them if they cried out or were a long time in giving birth. With no pain relievers of any kind, unless a Doctor was there to administer a little chloroform, women just had to sweat it out. Fortunately I knew a very good Midwife, who was free just then, so she attended me.

Soon after my baby's birth the Health Visitor called in to see if I needed any help or advice and to weigh the baby with her little spring balance. She was friendly and kind and I thanked her for her offer but as my baby was doing well and a friend had lent me her baby scales, I didn't need her help. She wore a uniform of navy blue hat and coat and rode about on a bicycle.

There was now a baby clinic in Banbury, held one afternoon a week where the babies were weighed and measured and advice given on any problems.. Several of my neighbours enjoyed going with their babies dressed in their best and having cups of tea and a chat to the other mothers. I didn't go as my baby was very active and lively and would soon have been bored sitting indoors in the clinic. Instead I took her for long walks in her pram, which we both enjoyed.

XIX 'Is There Anybody There?'

During the War years the garden at 113 Middleton Road, like the house, had grown rather shabby. Miss Welford had done her best to keep it tidy and the trees pruned after her father died but it needed attention. We were not great gardeners but did our best. I could cook and as we were so hard up, with so many mouths to feed, we made the most of the produce we could grow in the garden. Charles repaired the greenhouse, filling it with tomato plants which yielded a huge crop and he also grew quantities of vegetables. I couldn't do much gardening but the children were wonderful and worked very hard helping him. They picked the bumper crops of gooseberries, currants and strawberries, which we ate or I bottled, or made into jam with any sugar I could spare. I managed to do enough jam and fruit to last almost a year and pickled and bottled all I could.

James's Orange Blenheims and Bramley Seedlings had grown into huge trees and were laden with fruit and as we had no ladders, only a pair of steps, the only way to pick the fruit was for Charles and our eldest daughter Helen to climb up the trees with a basket. She was small and light and could climb like a cat and used to shin up the big trees with her basket to pick the fruit. Our bull terrier Rom also joined in the fruit picking, being fond of fruit herself. She picked strawberries and plums and pears from the lowest branches of the espalier trees and when there were fallers she always ate too many and had diarrhoea.

The American Redwood which James had planted beside the summer house had grown into a huge tree which could be seen from nearly all over Grimsbury. The summer house was as good as ever and the children loved it. Every summer they had their beds in it and slept out in the garden all night. When George was nine months old he joined them, sleeping in his cot beside their beds. Although Rom hated sleeping out she always accompanied them so she could mount guard and see they were all safe. She was a wonderful dog and was devoted to us all and was like a member of the family. We were all dreadfully upset when she died aged fifteen but George, who was four, was inconsolable and grieved for her for weeks.

Apart from Banbury Fair, the other highlights of the year to which the whole family would go were the Corpus Christi Procession and the Boxing Day Meet outside the Whately Hall Hotel. Corpus Christi was a Catholic event held at St. John's Church, South Bar. The procession of the Blessed Sacrament was held in conjunction with the celebration of the Feast of Corpus Christi. It took place on one of the first two Sunday evenings in June. It was an annual event, inaugurated by Father Brabazin, in 1922 and was continued until the early 1960's when the volume of traffic made it impossible to hold the event with safety. It was a lovely sight to see the huge procession emerging from St. John's Church, wending its way down South Bar to Banbury Cross and back, with everyone singing as they proceeded.

The procession was led by the Mace bearer dressed in black, the Cross bearer and Acolytes, their surplices trimmed with altar lace, followed by the choir and thurlers. Then came tiny girls in white with white veils on their heads, carrying baskets of rose petals. They strewed the petals in the path of the Blessed Host which was carried by the Priest, who wore beautifully embroidered robes, walking under a silken canopy carried by four parishioners. On either side of the Priest walked Guards of Honour carrying lighted candles. Next came the children of Mary and the May Queen, with her attendants. They were dressed all in white, with white veils and wreaths of flowers on their heads. The girls were followed by four young men, in surplices trimmed with altar lace, carrying the Statue of the Virgin Mary. The Sisters and pupils of Saint John's Priory came next, followed by the Catholic Guilds, carrying banners depicting various Saints. I can remember some of the Guilds' names: The Catholic Women's Guild, the Union of Catholic Mothers and the Catholic Young Men's Society. A large body of the general congregation brought up the rear. Just after the War, German prisoners of War from Bodicote joined in the procession.

The procession was one of the highlights in Banbury's year. Crowds thronged South Bar and around Banbury Cross to watch. When I was a child, my friends and I always watched and my own children were just as enthusiastic. Some years it must have rained and the procession cancelled, but I only remember warm and sunny Sunday evenings. The next event was on Boxing Day. Crowds of people would turn out to watch the colourful spectacle of the Hunt meeting outside the Whately Hall Hotel in the Horsefair and drinking sherry and hot toddies. The Whately Hall Hotel stands on the site of a very old inn – the Three Tuns. Over the years the old inn was altered and extended until it is the imposing building you see today. Like Corpus Christi the meet was later abandoned as the horses became frightened by the volume of traffic. I'm not in favour of blood sports but it was an impressive sight to see the beautiful horses and elegant ladies and bluff old colonels. The story goes that Colonel North from Wroxton could always rely on his horse taking him home if he became a little the worse for wear!

For some time Charles and I had been interested in Spiritualism and Psychic Research and with three friends had started a small circle, meeting once a week to see if we could get any 'psychic phenomena'. We had no results. We therefore decided to engage mediums to come and give demonstrations for us and invite anyone else who was interested.

We managed to buy a second-hand carpet for the sitting room, borrowed some chairs from my mother and were all set for our first meeting. Only a few people came. We hadn't been able to find a medium but one of our 'circle' asked a man to give a talk and demonstration on horoscopes and birth signs. It was wonderfully interesting and although the man had come all the way from Oxford he made no charge as astrology was his hobby.

Next we answered an advertisement in the magazine 'Psychic News', from a man who offered to give demonstrations of mediumship, anywhere close enough to Windsor for him to get there and back again on Tuesdays only. His name was Russell Harwood. The night of the meeting was terribly foggy and once again there were only a handful of people. We waited and waited and decided the man wasn't coming as it was past seven o'clock – then he turned up. There had been an accident and for hours his train had been shunting up and down outside Banbury.

He was a funny looking little man, in a shabby old suit which was much too big and sleeves which hung down well below his hands. We weren't impressed. But we soon changed our minds when he started his demonstration. He not only gave messages and accurate descriptions but names, addresses and dates to people in the meeting, from their dead relatives and friends. It was most impressive. We ourselves hardly knew the people who received the messages and the little man certainly couldn't have known them.

After the meeting he had to rush straight off to the station to catch his train to Windsor. He worked in a shop in Windsor and Tuesday was his afternoon off. He was obviously hard up but he wouldn't accept any fee – only let us pay his train fare. We tried to get him to come again, but he didn't answer our letters. He became a well known medium and when we met him years afterwards he told us that he had been involved in two more train accidents directly after the one in Banbury, which had made him too nervous to travel by train again.

With the advent of the cold weather it wasn't practical to hold any more meetings for a long while. When it was warmer the children moved to rooms at the top of the house leaving the back bedroom free. We held meetings again, which we financed by asking the five circle members to pay a shilling a week each into a small fund towards expenses. A woman who was interested in the meetings gave us some benches, we bought chairs cheap from the Midland Marts auction and of course my mother lent us any extra chairs. Gradually more and more people came until forty or fifty people were packing into our back bedroom for each meeting, with mediums coming to us from all over the country, among them Harold Sharpe.

Charles and I often had to accommodate the mediums overnight. We had plenty of room but no bedroom furniture, so my mother gave us some she didn't need, to furnish a comfortable bedroom for the mediums. We only could give them rough and ready hospitality but they didn't seem to mind and always wanted to come again. Some only came for a night but others stayed for several days to give private sittings or to take groups for demonstrations of clairvoyance. They charged a pound for an hour's private sitting and for a group of eight people, 2s 6d each, giving half to us for our expenses fund. Although some were famous mediums, none of them charged more than a pound for taking a meeting, with many of them just coming for the price of their train or bus fare.

They were a strange mixture of people. There were the well educated and sophisticated and then those who were almost illiterate and a small number who were just plain peculiar. The quality of mediumship varied enormously; some so poor it was embarrassing, while others gave remarkable evidence of survival. But one thing they all had in common was their utter sincerity. Entertaining the mediums was very hard work but Charles and I enjoyed it immensely. After the meetings when we had all had supper, Charles and I would sit up very late talking to them, hearing about their experiences and early lives. We learnt a great deal from them.

The meetings were going very well when suddenly I felt that we should cancel that summer's meetings. Everyone was disappointed. But it was as well we cancelled, because at the beginning of May, Anne had mumps. None of the family had had mumps but at regular intervals of the month, one after the other, we came down with them. When I was struck I didn't go to bed as there was no one to nurse me or look after the children. I stayed indoors keeping warm, going to bed as soon as Charles got home from work. Doctor Wharton however was so cross that I wouldn't go to bed, he refused to come and see me but asked Doctor Anne Davies to call in every day to see that we were all right.

It was the end of August and – a heatwave. We thought we had finally come to the end of the mumps, when Charles came down with them and was very ill for six weeks. Doctor Wharton sometimes had to call in twice a day. As it was so hot upstairs, we brought his bed down to the dining room and had the French windows to the garden wide open so he could get some air. He was often delirious and Doctor Wharton said I must stay up with him at night. But one night I was so tired I went upstairs, only meaning to lie down for a little while but fell into a deep sleep. That night Charles saw a dark shape at the end of the garden which was moving slowly towards the house. It turned into a big tiger which came walking through the French windows. It had a huge head and flashing eyes and stood looking down at him. Poor Charles was terrified and kept calling to me to come and help him but I remained fast asleep upstairs and didn't hear. Finally the beast disappeared. It took Charles a long while to get better and to forgive me!

As we were often asked about books to read on Spiritualism and Psychic Research, we decided to try and start a small library. We put an advert in the Psychic News asking for unwanted books. The response was amazing. We were overwhelmed with two or three hundred books. I went and saw Mr Jackson the Antique Dealer, who sold me a very large, solid oak bookcase cheap, for twenty pounds, which I paid for out of the fund. It reached from the floor to the ceiling, just fitting into the corner of our dining room.

Soon after we had the library set up we gave a tea party in the dining room and about ten of us were squashed round the table by the bookcase. After the party I asked Charles if there was something the matter with the floor as it felt so springy. He went down to the basement to investigate and found there was hardly anything supporting the floors – the joists were eaten away with dry rot. It was a miracle the floor hadn't given way and landed us and the bookcase into the basement. As usual we had no money, but a retired carpenter, who was a regular attender at our meetings, offered to repair the floor for nothing, if Charles bought the timber and helped him with the work.

For a short while we had no more disasters until one night there was a terrible thunderstorm which lasted all night. There were great flashes of blue and purple lightning – the thunder crashing directly over our heads. Charles and I were nervous but the children were terrified. We sat all together in our big bed waiting for the storm to pass when suddenly there was a tremendous noise and the house shook. In the morning we found that one of our big chimney stacks had been struck by lightning and most of the slates from the roof had been ripped off. Once again our insurance paid out. It was a good thing because the damage was considerable.

Our next trouble came soon after the storm, when the old hot water tank in the airing cupboard collapsed. The bottom had corroded away and floods of rusty water poured all over our blankets and sheets. It did a great deal of damage but this time the insurance company wouldn't pay as the tank was so old.

Things went on fairly calmly for quite a while, until the next August Bank Holiday. Charles was away from home and Helen and little Charles, 'Tarka', were away at Quaker Summer School, leaving only George, Anne and myself at home. I hadn't been down the basement for some days but I had to go down for something that afternoon. I was horrified to find that the basement floor was awash with sewage. I didn't know what to do.

I shut Anne and George upstairs in the front bedroom so they should be out of the smell and went up the road and looked for John Grant the builder. He came at once and he prised up the stone slab that covered the manhole cover in the basement and found that it was blocked solid. It was what is called an old tumbling bay, not like a modern manhole at all. It worked quite efficiently provided nothing blocked it, but ours was hopelessly blocked. We dug a great big hole in the garden, John went and got a gadget like a giant soup ladle and we collected the buckets of sewage. John filled, and I emptied them into the hole in the garden. It was a terrible job and the smell was frightful and it took ages to clear. John was very good. As soon as we had done that and the cellar had been swilled down and dried off, he built a proper modern manhole so we didn't have any more trouble with the drains.

I think that was the end of our big disasters. We just had smaller things which seemed a piece of cake after that. But our financial position was very rocky. We decided to take lodgers to see if we could get a little extra money. Our lodgers were two very nice ladies, who had the two bedrooms at the top of the house, with the use of our sitting room, leaving us the dining room and the kitchen, two bedrooms for the children and our own big front bedroom. We still carried on with the meetings every month. But it was not the same when we no longer had the house to ourselves. For one thing, we couldn't give the mediums overnight accommodation. When it was summer, it was not too bad because the children liked to sleep out in the summer-house and the medium could have one of their bedrooms. But in the winter, my mother was a brick and she would give the mediums a bed for the night. But it was not the same. We missed the friendly atmosphere and the talks after supper. Finally we gave up taking lodgers as I realised we were working very hard and earning very little money.

23. *Boxing Day Meet outside the Whately Hall Hotel, Horsefair.*

24. *Banbury Town Hall, Cow Fair.*

XX *Over Here*

It was about this time that the Americans were being stationed at Heyford and Croughton USAF bases. Our financial position still being precarious, we decided that as the servicemen wanted accommodation and we wanted the cash, to take advantage and make a flat at the top of our house. This was to change the course of our lives.

It proved a disaster for our spiritualist meetings. In shuffling our family around the house to make way for the new flat, we left ourselves only two bedrooms for the four children, the big front bedroom for ourselves and our sitting room, dining room and kitchen, with no room for meetings. It wasn't too bad being so confined but having strangers tramping up and down the house was dreadful. Some of our tenants we liked very much. The first ones were a very nice couple with a little boy. But the wife suffered from insomnia and would get up in the night deciding to bake cakes! She had a very noisy hand whisk and used to crash about in her kitchen, which was over our bedroom – the noise nearly driving us mad. Their little boy also was a pest as he was dreadfully spoilt and he was always trying to move in on us.

Also at this time, we had bought a share in a house with a friend. He lived in a third of it, letting the other two parts to American servicemen. Of course Charles and I had taken out a big loan along with our building society loan on our home. Our income from the rents was not enough to cover the outgoings. Charles and I were once again in a monetary mess.

This time we took a terrible plunge and let our dining-room as a bed-sitting room. It was the end of all things. It only left us the kitchen to sit and eat our meals. We had a nice sitting-room but as we liked to entertain, only having a kitchen was a real hardship. However while our finances improved, our garden became our salvation and refuge. We loved it. But we wore it hard. We were not good gardeners, not knowing how to prune trees or renew plants. The bottom part of the garden was put to grass as a lawn was easier to maintain. We all spent hours in the garden, just to escape the barrage of people occupying the house. The garden may have looked shabby but it was a haven.

Meanwhile our psychic phenomena meetings had retreated to the basement. It wasn't too bad. But we liked to have music at our meetings and as there was no way we could have a radiogram in the basement, we bribed the children to put on records for us, which they took turns in doing. We selected the records we wanted played and by a signal of banging on the ceiling with the handle of a broom, the children upstairs – whoever was on duty – would make a change of records. The children were dreadfully embarrassed with our activities. They didn't like to invite their friends to the house when we were holding a meeting, as they felt that we and our friends were so weird. It was difficult to explain why a group of adults were sitting in a basement in the dark, making strange noises, listening to music and banging on the floor with a broom handle!

Ever since he had been demobilised from the Army, Charles had worked for his father in his bookmaking business. They had constant arguments and quarrels, never seeing eye to eye. One day their quarrel was more serious than usual and Charles walked out. He was out of work for two or three weeks until he was offered a job at Aluminium Laboratories, in the photographic department. The job would often take him away from home for several days but Charles found it very rewarding and although he was only engaged to carry equipment and drive the van, Ken Blore and Bob Seaman were very good, training him to become a very efficient photographer.

Soon after Charles had taken his job at the Labs, our youngest child was born in 1954, a dear little girl. We called her Sylvia. She was quite a bit younger than the other members of the family and they were all very fond of her and made a great pet of her. She was more difficult to bring up than the others as she was rather delicate and needed more care. We always joked that if she had been the first born, she would have been the last!

Life took another turn. Charles's father died. He left him sole legatee to his estate, as Charles was his only son and heir. It eased our financial situation immediately. It left us in a quandary however, whether to restore our present house or look for another. We certainly needed more room. With five children and now a grandchild (Helen our eldest had married but her husband was in the RAF and stationed overseas, so she continued to live at home) ourselves, the family pets, let alone all our tenants – we were packed like sardines. We decided we would look for a new house. We felt that the atmosphere of our home had been completely ruined with all the flats and different people who had been living in it. Our circle also had broken up at this time as the members felt that now we were financially better off things would not be the same. Charles and I were terribly upset by our circle's reasoning and it became another reason why we decided to move away and make a completely new start.

We lived at 113 Middleton Road from 1946 to 1958. They were very happy years, in spite of all our difficulties and trials, and I think I would say that some of those years were the happiest of our lives.

My parents were still living at 107 Middleton Road. During the War they had dug up the lawn and all the flowers and tried to grow vegetables. It wasn't a success, as the shade from the trees made the vegetables long and spindly. The pond sprung a bad leak and had to be filled in and the little threepenny and sixpenny goldfish which had grown so large, my father had managed to sell, for ten pounds each, to the Aluminium Company for their ornamental fish pond.

After the War the house and garden were once again becoming derelict and neglected. The summer-house had fallen down, the wash-house had lost most of its slates, the little greenhouse was falling to bits and the outside toilet was hopelessly blocked up. My father and mother were not getting any younger. The house was too big for them and they couldn't afford the upkeep. To help with the expenses they had turned the first and second floors into two flats, letting them to American servicemen and their wives. It kept them solvent for a while, but eventually they couldn't cope any longer.

We decided to move and my parents to come with us. We were lucky enough to buy 4 West Bar, at the other end of the town, a house belonging to the Quaker family of Braithwaites. As usual it was far too big for us, and far too expensive but we loved it and were determined to live there. For my mother and father we made a flat in part of the house. My mother, however, never got over leaving Grimsbury and was always heart-broken at the wrench of twenty-five years of memory. My father, was glad to be rid of the worry of bills and trying to keep pace with never-ending repairs.

We decided not to sell our old homes of 107 and 113 Middleton Road, but keep them converted as flats, continuing to let them and drawing an income. After much soul-searching Charles retired from The Laboratories and decided to go self-employed, as I was finding it difficult to run the family home and maintain the letting business, as he would be away from home days at a time. And besides which, we had plans to make a real go of the business.

The gardens of the houses, as I have explained, were very long, extending to South Street. By some means we had raised all sorts of mortgages and loans, obtained planning permission and were going to erect purpose-built blocks of flats on the gardens. I remember what a terrible wrench it was when it came to the moment of truth. The gardens had to be cleared, the trees cut down, the summer-houses, greenhouse and ponds all levelled, all gone. I hadn't got the heart to go anywhere near it until the shell of the flats was completely up, as it was too heart-breaking. I just had to think of other things. The children never went near it again for years. It was like destroying an old friend. Charles knew nothing about building but he learnt. We employed a sub-contractor to build the flats which we had designed. For our building supplies Charles would go to Hoods, Dalbys and other builder's merchants in the town. Everyone was always most helpful in giving advice on the best nails and best bricks and paint. Hoods, even if you weren't buying anything, was always worth a visit.

Hoods at 35 and 36 Bridge Street, was a wonderful shop selling every kind of ironmongery you could think of. The shop was large and rambling, made up of some old houses which had been linked together as the shop expanded. There were three entrance doors, two of which had narrow double doors with etched glass engraved panels let into them. The store-rooms and workshops were in all sorts of unexpected places, all over the building and often up staircases. The floors were uneven and rickety with metal patches nailed over the holes, low ceilings and cobwebs. In some of the remoter store-rooms the stocks had been there for years and were antique. If you wanted anything old or unusual Hoods was the place to go. They also had large comprehensive stocks of modern ironmongery.

It was owned by Mr W. S. Orchard, a small dark man who always wore black clothes and a black Derby hat. He was a wealthy man, treated his employees well, was charming, had an eye for the ladies and was a well-known and liked character in the town. He also owned Dalbys Timber Merchants Yard at Bridge Street and several other properties in the town. He lived next to Hoods, at 37 Bridge Street. This was a beautiful old stone house set well back from the road partially screened from the passers-by by iron railings, shrubs and large trees. A flagstone path led from the front gate up to the house which was quiet and mysterious looking. I always wished I could have lived there. Unfortunately it was demolished to make way for the very, very, boring shopping precinct.

Mr Orchard like most of his family was unmarried. One of his sisters was the Miss Orchard who was engaged for fourteen years to William Potts, editor of the Banbury Guardian. The family home was West Beech Court, in West Bar. A fine house with a huge garden and orchard, on which West Beech Court flats and the Trades and Labour

Club car park are built. Inside, the big rooms had marble fireplaces and ornate plaster ceilings. A large staircase, with a big glass chandelier hanging above it, swept up from the hall.

When the eldest brother, Mr T. Orchard and two sisters were left at home, the sisters bought a nice but much smaller house in Oxford Road. But their eldest brother refused to move and lived on in the old house alone. His poor sisters had to go up and down from Oxford Road every day to get his dinner and do his housework. This elder brother also owned a great deal of land and a number of houses in West Bar. The College is built on land he owned. He was a wealthy man but very unpopular as he was grim and domineering and some townspeople called him the 'Old Gorilla'.

It was a sad day when Hoods became modernised to make way for the shopping precinct. The shop had a 'closing down' sale before it was demolished. People came from miles around to buy obscure fixtures and fittings no longer made, tools, kitchen equipment, everything fascinating, covered in dust, hidden in corners. Now all screws and nails come pre-packaged and you no longer can buy one screw or one nail. Hoods, though, is still there but now in a modern purpose-built building and its stock has lost its charm.

Overlooking Hoods is Banbury Town Hall.

Banbury Town Hall was the hub of town life. All the business of the town was conducted there. There was the police station; the magistrates' court; the lock-ups on the ground floor; the public toilets in the basement; the rates office; the council chambers, where all the council meetings were held. The Mayor's inauguration ceremony and banquet were held there, also town proclamations, declared either from the balcony or from the large double doors leading from the town hall steps, exhibitions, lectures – indeed all social, administrative or educational events.

Whenever there was a new town Mayor there was great festivity. The Mayoress would hold, what was called an 'at home', an afternoon tea for the local ladies. The catering would be supervised, as a rule, by Browns Cake Shop. Browns would provide the best china, silver teapots and tea urns, with the tea laid out on beautiful white table-cloths. The Mayor's Banquet, invitation only, was a very grand and prestigious affair. Chapmans, the best local furnishing shop, would provide drapes for the windows, gilt chairs and little tables, carpets for the main room, red carpeting for the stairs and corridors, decorations, flowers, potted palms and long dining tables with snowy white cloths. Music would also be provided, either by Mr Webb or Mr Chidzey's orchestra. The caterers, again would usually be Browns, though the other local firms could take a turn. Food was a nightmare to prepare as the kitchens were obsolete and situated in the basement. The food would have to be kept hot and rushed to the first floor where the party was being held. It was always a frantic rush as there were so many people to serve. The present day Mayoral celebrations seem to have lost favour, with the Mayors having to advertise in the local paper trying to 'sell' tickets for their inaugural dinners.

I was never invited to any, but the grandest event of the year, was the annual Hunt Ball – invitation limited to only members of the Hunt and their friends. Chapmans would be employed again for the furnishing and decoration, which they would take especial care of – providing easy chairs and small sofas – the very best.

I worked for Browns, who would undertake the catering, excelling their usual high standards with the cooks from the big houses providing extra food for the evening; dainties such as caviare and canapés. The County families would also send their servants along, the butlers, the maids and the ladies' maids to wait on the guests in the cloakrooms and at the dining table. In the cloakrooms there would be dressing-tables, sofas, powder, towels, luxury soap and even smelling salts for those feeling a little faint.

The members of the Hunt, dressed either in pink or tails and the ladies in evening dress and their parties of friends, would dance to 4 am to a top band of the day hired from London. A riotous affair. The last dance of the evening would be a noisy Post-Horn Gallop. At the close of the Ball, soup would be provided for all the guests as they left.

The event that immediately followed the Hunt Ball was the Hospital Ball, which was held the following evening so as to take advantage of the Hunt Ball's decorations and furnishings. Again by invitation only, this however was a very sober affair, after the excitement of the previous night. The Matron of the hospital would issue the invitations to all senior doctors and nurses and professional medical people of the town, such as the dentists. Chiropodists were not considered to be high enough up the medical social ladder to attend! There was a film made recently called 'A Private Function' which was making the same point.

The Farmers Ball, however, I did go to. Tickets had to be bought well in advance as it was so popular being a rowdy, jolly affair. The close of the evening would be a boisterous Post Horn Gallop. It was great fun. The other dances I went to were those of the Northern Aluminium Social Club. Weekly dances were held and though humdrum, they were very cheap and very popular with no formal evening dress required.

Cecil Sharp came to the Town Hall once, to give a demonstration of country dancing and folk songs. He was famous as a collector of traditional songs and dances, going round the country rescuing old songs and recording traditions, before they should be forgotten. Mr Sharp came into Browns Cake Shop when my father was working there and Bill Bennett, the head of the bakehouse, would sing all the old songs he knew to him. The demonstration given in the Town Hall was quite remarkable. Cecil Sharp would play the piano and fiddle, to accompany an extraordinary group of female dancers. With today's fashions I'm sure nobody would bat an eye lid but in those days it was really something to watch these tall, thin women dressed in plain, white cotton dresses, open-work sandals and bandanas tied around their heads. I'm not quite sure what we all made of it! With hindsight it was wonderful to be able to say we witnessed it.

The Winter Lectures were another popular event held at the Town Hall. Wonderful speakers came to Banbury. There were members of the Everest and Antarctic expeditions and writers such as H. G. Wells, Hugh Walpole and John Drinkwater. Sometimes Lord North was the Chairman of the Winter Lectures and would entertain the visiting speaker at his home at Wroxton Abbey. Lord North would arrive late at the Town Hall for the lecture, after partaking of a good dinner and good wines. I'm afraid that I and the other younger members of the audience would be more interested in Lord North and would watch him as he teetered about on the stage in the hopes that he would fall off the platform.

The Town Hall would also host photographic exhibitions, arts and crafts work of school children, amateur theatricals, music recitals, private parties and dances – but they would be rather bleak as the Town Hall was large and needed the carpets and crowds of people to make it jolly.

Decorating the main function room were good mahogany benches, seats and tables. On the walls hung wonderful, valuable Old Master oil paintings of such people as Prince Rupert. There were also portraits of all the Mayors of the town and Lord North. I remember there was a scandal about where the furnishings and valuable paintings had gone, with the local people writing letters but I don't know what the outcome was.

Today Banbury has no heart and the Town Hall hosts mostly one day bargain sales of leather coats, and cheap oil paintings from Taiwan. It is not the place it was.

In my painting I have shown a Midland Red bus (the bus station was later situated there) and some of the many small shops which were around the outskirts of the building. There was a funny Victorian shop, up a flight of steps, a tobacconist, run by Mr Hutt, brother of Jackie Hutt of Calthorpe Street. Also there was a sweet shop run by one of the Leach family, a photographers and watch and clock repairer, John Bonham. They have all gone and the building has been modernised to house another bank.

XXI These Golden Days I Spend With You

And it's a long long while from May to December,
And the days grow short when you reach September,
And the Autumn weather turns the leaves to flame,
And I haven't got time for the waiting game,
For the days dwindle down to a precious few – September, November,
And these few precious days I spend with you,
These golden days I spend with you.

September Song, Anderson-Weill

This song was popular in my youth and seems to sum up my feelings and mood of the book. Writing my story of personal memories of how I saw Banbury has been very nostalgic and rather sad. The buildings, businesses and community spirit that was in the town have long gone. It is a town of impersonal banks, building societies and estate agents. The local tradesman offering a service to the community is a thing of the past. I believe that nationwide that there are only 2,000 independent retailers left and all shops now are chain stores. Every week in the Banbury Guardian one reads about yet another shop closing down. It is all very sad.

My memories were begun originally as a keepsake for my family – gossip and recollections – nothing more serious, but I was persuaded that there was a wider audience who wanted to know more about Banbury, not just about ancient history and a lot of dates.

My first book 'Memories of Banbury' brought forth many letters from all over the World from people who had lived in Banbury at one time or another, and the special affection they felt for the place. It was this enthusiasm and the demand for a sequel that has brought this book about.

I was brought up a Quaker but I had never consciously thought about the tremendous impact they had in their community and what a tight-knit group they were, with connections all around the country. I hope that James Cadbury, Misses Browns, Joseph and Beatrice Gillett and the many others will receive some recognition or remembrance today. They worked tirelessly to help others achieve a better quality of life and I'm sure they would be shocked that the reforms which they fought so hard to achieve have been exploited and misused by those who scrounge from the system, who never intend to work and feel the State owes them a living.

In recalling my memories of my family and my husband's family, my daughter Sylvia remarked how very dull, unremarkable and conventional their descendants have become. It's true – both sides of our families, were thick with flamboyant personalities, who travelled, took risks and were fascinating, exceptional people, not all of them pleasant by any means but certainly not people to pass without trace.

I have written about times of great poverty and hardship but there was a lot of friendship. You could leave your front doors open, walk down the street at night and not worry if your children were playing in the park alone. It has become a book of how people from impossible backgrounds managed to rise above their problems and achieve success. My father, Robert Pursaill, who was illiterate and had a cockney accent, which was an enormous social stigma, educated himself, lost his accent and helped people at Uffculme Hospital, and held a responsible job at Brown's cake shop. Many people who lived in Calthorpe Street became successful and respected. My husband's family who achieved so much from nothing. . . .

Banbury has a history of demolishing beautiful buildings, dating back to the Civil War, when Banbury Castle was pulled down. The shopping precinct is on the Castle foundations. I have yet to meet anyone who doesn't comment about the number of buildings and historical places that Banbury allows to be demolished, even when the town voices disapproval.

My husband and I have now retired and sold all our properties in Grimsbury to a Housing Association and to private individuals. It was a relief to sell them as it was becoming a great strain to maintain them. It is still sad to think of the gardens that have gone. We are still living in our house that we bought 35 years ago and we are now among the last residents in the neighbourhood. The other houses have been turned into offices and the gardens into car parks.

I am nearly 80 and I never dreamed I could produce one book, let alone two. I have difficulty writing a postcard. But it was the encouragement and interest that I received that made me continue. I wish to thank all those who have supplied photographic memories, personal memories or verified the information in this book. You are all too numerous to mention and I'd hate to miss out a name – so I thank you all. It is written in many books and believe me it is a true statement – thank you to my family who have put up with me in completing this book. And especially to my daughter Sylvia and my husband Charles who have nagged and cajoled. My memories are not exhausted and there are memories too sensational which can't be printed – at least not until 50 years after my death! I hope you have enjoyed these golden days which I have spent with you.